Don
Happy Vesting!
Kate

VESTED

VESTED

HOW P&G, McDONALD'S AND MICROSOFT ARE REDEFINING WINNING IN BUSINESS RELATIONSHIPS

KATE VITASEK and KARL MANRODT
with
JEANNE KLING

palgrave
macmillan

VESTED
Copyright © Kate Vitasek and Karl Manrodt, 2012.
All rights reserved.

First published in 2012 by PALGRAVE MACMILLAN® in the
United States—a division of St. Martin's Press LLC, 175 Fifth Avenue,
New York, NY 10010.

Where this book is distributed in the UK, Europe and the rest of the world,
this is by Palgrave Macmillan, a division of Macmillan Publishers Limited,
registered in England, company number 785998, of Houndmills,
Basingstoke, Hampshire RG21 6XS.

Palgrave Macmillan is the global academic imprint of the above companies
and has companies and representatives throughout the world.

Palgrave® and Macmillan® are registered trademarks in the United States,
the United Kingdom, Europe and other countries.

ISBN 978-0-230-34170-8

Library of Congress Cataloging-in-Publication is available at the
Library of Congress

A catalogue record of the book is available from the British Library.

Cover and Jacket design by Elizabeth Kanna and Kristopher Bazen

Text design by Newgen Imaging Systems, Ltd., Chennai, India

First edition: September 2012

D 10 9 8 7 6 5 4 3 2

Printed in the United States of America.

We would like to dedicate this book to our spouses, who have selflessly given us time, support, and encouragement throughout our careers. We are firsthand believers that win-win principles are a foundation for success in our personal lives. Our marriages are a testament that together is indeed better.

Greg, Susan, and Steven, we are in your debt and appreciate all that you have done for us. We look forward with love to being together for many years to come.

Greg Picinich,
Vested to Kate Vitasek since May 17, 2003

Susan Manrodt,
Vested to Karl Manrodt since June 12, 1982

Steven Kling,
Vested to Jeanne Kling since February 24, 1990

CONTENTS

INTRODUCTION

A meme is an idea that behaves like a virus—that moves through a population, taking hold in each person it infects.

—*Malcolm Gladwell*

The Air Force was curious. And so were we.

Was there a better way to outsource? What began as a research project to find a better way for the Air Force to buy services, from logistics support for weapon systems to facilities and operational services for its bases, has evolved into a powerful concept: a concept we have coined *Vested*.

Companies choosing a Vested approach work in a highly strategic manner with their business partners—whether they are suppliers, customers, stakeholders, or employees. But they go well beyond simply saying they have a strategic relationship. Our research revealed these very successful business relationships follow five core principles that are so fundamental to their success we think of them as inviolable rules. This book goes behind the scenes of some of the best business relationships we uncovered in our research. We reveal how the best of the best are following the Vested rules—and, as a result, are redefining how to develop winning business relationships in the twenty-first century.

EVOLUTION

Our original research—a collaboration among the University of Tennessee (UT), the United States Air Force, and the Defense Acquisition University—studied some of the world's most successful outsourcing relationships. The goal was simple: Find a better way to outsource services.

Our initial work uncovered some wildly successful government services contracts and others that failed to achieve basic cost and service performance. Just how did the Department of Energy turn a Cold War plutonium production plant into a wildlife refuge when the General Accountability Office gave it less than a 1 percent chance of success? And how was General Electric able to overhaul the Navy's spare parts planning and engine maintenance process for the F/A-18 Hornet? The overhaul led to dramatic results, including reducing repair turnaround time from 120 to 47 days, raising component availability from 50 to 92 percent, and reducing the fleet's total cost of ownership by $79 million.

Many argue that it is easy to make such large improvements because the government is often inefficient. With that in mind, we expanded our research to the commercial sector, unpacking how Procter & Gamble (P&G), McDonald's, Microsoft, and companies like them approached their most successful outsourcing relationships. Surely the commercial sector has dynamic and ever-changing business requirements, just like the Air Force. Was there something the Air Force could learn to become more effective at spending taxpayers' dollars?

Through UT's research efforts, we studied companies that achieved transformational, game-changing, and award-winning results. Some of the relationships were new. Others had been in place over 50 years.

What did these organizations have in common? Could we codify them and teach others how to replicate their success?

NAVIGATION INTRODUCTION xi

What we found were radically different types of business relationships. Relationships that transcended traditional buy-sell transaction-based thinking typically focused on the lowest price or operational performance targets through service-level agreements. Relationships that inspired innovation, created value, and rewarded success. Relationships that were, well, Vested in their very nature.

In all cases, companies had a conscious focus on the relationship itself and a commitment to maximize the value for everyone. Together, the parties believed that 1 + 1 could equal 3, 4, or even more. Instead of looking at how each individual company achieves its goals (What's In It For Me, or WIIFMe), the parties (yes, it could be many!) focused on WIIFWe, or What's In It For *We*.

By so doing, they achieved true win-win relationships.

Our research found that these relationships followed five principles. These principles, which we came to refer to as rules, create a competitive advantage for the organizations and are an inviolable part of how the companies work together.

But what good are rules without a way of applying them to your situation?

Our initial research led us to create a systematic methodology to improve outsourcing as a business practice. We called our approach Vested Outsourcing® because the core principle centers on creating outsourcing relationships where companies and their suppliers become Vested in each other's success. The partners make a conscious effort to drive benefits for both the company that is outsourcing and its service providers.

Our research was poised to resonate with buyers, suppliers, lawyers, academics and industry thought leaders and spread fast.

In fact, the Vested methodology received accolades from longtime outsourcing leaders such as Frank Casale—chief executive officer of the Outsourcing Institute—who stated, "Vested Outsourcing is a game-changing approach that will quickly become the new gold standard for advanced outsourcing relationships."[1] The International Association of Outsourcing Professionals quickly endorsed the UT's executive education course on Vested Outsourcing as part of its Certified Outsourcing Professional™ program.

In February 2010, we released our first book on the topic—*Vested Outsourcing: Five Rules That Will Transform Outsourcing*. It described our initial research conducted for the Air Force and outlined our Vested Five Rules to building relationships. In less than 20 months, it was in its seventh printing.

We were excited to see companies embracing the concept of Vested. However, practitioners expressed a real need, almost a yearning, to have a step-by-step road map to help them create Vested agreements that followed the Five Rules.

Once again we turned to collaboration to expand our research, this time teaming with the International Association for Contract and Commercial Management to create a follow-up book—*The Vested Outsourcing Manual: A Guide for Creating Successful Business and Outsourcing Agreements*—published in June 2011.

The goal of the manual? To serve as a how-to guide for companies to develop Vested agreements that allow them to move beyond merely paying lip service to the idea of a strategic partnership and embed the Vested Five Rules into contractual outsourcing agreements and governance structures. Leading experts and innovators have contributed to the evolution of Vested principles and the Vested business model. For *The Vested Outsourcing Manual,* we teamed with the renowned British deal maker Jacqui Crawford; the very progressive lawyer, mediator, arbitrator, and professional negotiations skill trainer Jeanette Nyden; and Katherine Kawamoto, the inquisitive and passionate vice president of research at the International Association for Contract and Commercial Management (IACCM).

Together, the team created a manual that teaches companies how to develop Vested agreements. The manual is based on the Vested Five Rules and the seminal work of the 2009 Nobel Laureate Dr. Oliver Williamson in transaction cost economics and economic governance. Dr. Williamson's research reveals companies need to develop contracts based on a "flexible framework." He encourages companies to work collaboratively and proactively to address their ever-changing business needs rather than to develop rigid and muscular processes that put suppliers in a box, with every change being out of scope and causing tensions.

Dawn Tiura Evans—chief executive of the professional association Sourcing Interest Group—and Jim Eckler from the Center of Outsource Research and Education immediately endorsed the collaborative and pioneering work of UT and IACCM. During this part of our work, we extended our collaborative relationship to include the Sourcing Interest Group and the Center for Outsource Research and Education and began exploring the Vested concept as a sourcing business model in more detail.

Simply put, organizations have tools available when they work with suppliers, and they need to use the right tools for the job. Vested is the right tool to develop strategic relationships that unlock hidden value and innovation.

Today, our work has moved well beyond buyer-supplier relationships. We have studied all types of business relationships across virtually every industry. What started out as the study of P&G's and Microsoft's award-winning outsourcing relationships evolved into studies of organizations that often do not even apply the word "outsourcing" to their own practices. Some of those we studied simply believed in finding strategic alliances that create long-term competitive advantage for both themselves and their partners.

We examined over a dozen of McDonald's most strategic supplier relationships—from farm to fork—and learned the company's secret for inspiring its suppliers to invest millions of dollars and years developing products and processes that create a sizable competitive advantage for restaurants under the Golden Arches.

We explored how the Minnesota Department of Transportation worked with Flatiron–Manson, FIGG Bridge Engineering, and Johnson Brothers to rebuild the I-35W Bridge in a record-setting 18 months after its collapse left the citizens of Minneapolis devastated by the loss of life and without a bridge.

We learned how a small business, Integrated Management Systems, provides innovative approaches for staffing that have improved worker productivity by up to 300 percent. Water For People, a nonprofit organization, seems to understand how to build sustainable and successful relationships that effectively eliminate water poverty in some of the world's poorest regions.

From burgers to bridges to small businesses and not-for-profits, the Vested Five Rules still applied. But our seven years of research did not just turn up good stories. What started as a research project transformed into a methodology and then a business model. It has evolved once more.

During the process of writing this book, we spent hundreds of hours interviewing people about their Vested relationships and documenting their stories—diving beneath the research and directly into the DNA. What we learned is that being Vested or using Vested thinking is much more than a progressive buyer-supplier relationship, a methodology, or even a business model. Vested is a choice—it is how you work with others in your ecosystem, whether they are your suppliers, your customers, or your employees.

People and companies that lack the Vested mind-set often consider Vested principles to be radical. Vested is not for everyone or for every situation. It is for those seeking trust, transparency, and transformation in how they manage key parts of their business.

We hope these stories will inspire you to follow a proven path to develop hyperproductive business relationships of your own. As you read the stories that follow, challenge yourself to answer this question: Just how Vested am I in the success of my business partners? If you do not have a Vested relationship, you are likely holding yourself, your suppliers, your employees, and possibly your entire organization back from achieving the kind of award-winning and transformational success we found in our cases studies.

The organizations profiled are part of a fast-growing movement—a movement of organizations with Vested relationships creating tremendous results by redefining winning. Great change is ahead.

1

VESTING FOR SUCCESS

To raise new questions, new possibilities, to regard old problems
from a new angle, requires creative imagination and marks real
advance.

—*Albert Einstein*

When A. G. Lafley took the helm as the chief executive
officer (CEO) of Procter & Gamble (P&G) in 2000,
he had grand visions to ensure the venerable consumer
packaged goods giant remained at the forefront of innovation
as it entered the twenty-first century. What came as a surprise
to industry watchers was not Lafley's focus on innovation but
how he planned on leading P&G to success. Lafley declared that
"half of our new products [will] come from our own labs, and
half would come through them."[1] He was willing to bet that
looking beyond P&G walls would enable the company to produce highly profitable innovations that would drive value for
both it and its partners.

A radical idea.

Lafley's strategy was not a call for the replacement of P&G
capabilities but rather for ways to better leverage P&G's core

strengths. His aggressive goals would require company-wide reinvention, not just in how P&G developed products but also in the way it managed its internal business operations. The direction from A. G. Lafley was clear: P&G needed to prioritize resources to concentrate on its core competencies of marketing and product development. P&G turned to Filippo Passerini to help lead the charge in transforming the company's internal operations. Passerini and his team would need to figure out how to achieve lower costs *and* higher service levels for P&G's internal shared services group known as the Global Business Services (GBS) organization.

"The time was ripe for making the move to outsource," explained Passerini. "By consolidating and standardizing our services, we...could leverage the greater scale and unique expertise of outsourcing partners. Our objective was to further cut costs *and* improve service levels. By outsourcing the more repetitive commodity work and keeping in-house only what we considered strategic, we could, in effect, enable ourselves to focus on innovation and developing new business capabilities for P&G."[2]

The end goal would require innovative solutions that would transform "overhead expense" into an entirely new entity. By the end of 2003, P&G had entered outsourcing partnerships in information technology infrastructure, finance and accounting, human resources, and facilities management worth $4.2 billion. P&G selected Jones Lang LaSalle (JLL), a global leader in real estate services, to manage the transformation of its facilitites management services in more than 60 countries.

Although P&G deems all of its outsourcing highly effective, the business relationship with JLL has been, by all factors, wildly successful. In just five short years, JLL went from being a new P&G supplier to winning "Supplier of the Year," a coveted honor awarded to a select few supplier partners annually. JLL was especially pleased to earn the title two years in a row—in 2008 and 2009—an extremely rare occurrence.

But just how did P&G and JLL do it?

Jon Chiglo remembers August 1, 2007, as if it were yesterday. Chiglo, a Minnesota Department of Transportation (MnDOT) employee, was enjoying a relaxing evening out at a local restaurant with friends. His wife, a photographer for local media, was a no-show. Missing her and wondering where she was, Jon gave her a call. "Oh, Jon," she apologized, "News just broke. The I-35W bridge collapsed in Minneapolis and I've been called back to work."

Chiglo stopped dead in his tracks. Bridges do not fall down. He went to the bar area where patrons were watching the Minnesota Twins play against the Kansas City Royals in the Hubert H. Humphrey Metrodome in Minneapolis. The stadium is located just west of I-35W, and public safety officials had decided it was better to continue the game, as postponement would mean sending up to 25,000 people back into traffic only blocks away from the collapsed bridge. As far as the bar sports fans were concerned, it was just a regular night.

Chiglo asked the restaurant workers to switch the TVs from the sports cable channel to news. The screens filled with images of broken concrete, car pileups, smoke, and emergency vehicles. The previously noisy bar fell silent as patrons joined Chiglo in disbelief. In Chiglo's words, "It was a nightmare. Not just for me as a MnDOT employee but for everyone. It was our worst nightmare."

MnDOT Bridge #9340 (known to locals as the I-35W Bridge) had buckled and then collapsed into the mighty Mississippi River 64 feet below. One hundred and eleven vehicles tumbled into the water; 17 cars were submerged, and many others were stranded on crumbling and fallen blocks of concrete. A semitrailer caught fire, as did several cars. A school bus carrying 63 children perched precariously against a guardrail. It was a dangerous and frightening situation.

In the end, 13 people—8 men and 5 women—died, and 145 others were injured.

On September 18, 2008—less than 18 months after the tragic collapse and much to the amazement of, well, just about everybody—the new, state-of-the-art St. Anthony Falls Bridge on I-35W opened for business. At 5:00 a.m., cars lined up for hours for the privilege of following first responders, state troopers, and MnDOT construction vehicles across the 1,223-foot span for the first time.

A typical bridge replacement takes at least five years. But MnDOT did it in less than 18 months and came in under budget. More than simply a replacement bridge, it is a breathtaking piece of architecture and technology that earned the 2009 Grand Prize of America's Transportation Awards for "representing the best in innovative management, accountability and timeliness."

But just how did MnDOT do it?

Patrick Malone lived in a teepee right smack over the railroad tracks leading into Rocky Flats nuclear production site for nine months in 1978. The teepee was home to Malone and a few of his fellow activists who wanted the site shut down. There was good reason for citizen outrage. People perceived nuclear production as dangerous and scary. Protesters wanted to get the attention of the Department of Energy (DOE) and the Environmental Protection Agency (EPA). In fact, they wanted to get the attention of anyone who would listen, and Malone's teepee was one of many strategies used.

The primary mission of Rocky Flats was to fabricate plutonium pits, which are the triggers for nuclear bombs. The cores are comprised of a "hollow plutonium shell about the size of a grapefruit. A typical one explodes with the force of around

20,000 tons of TNT."[3] Public concern began to grow after recurring plutonium fires in buildings 771 and 776 and traces of tritium (a radioactive form of hydrogen) were detected in the local water supply. Making matters worse, government agencies were feuding over who had control. Claiming "national security," DOE argued that Rocky Flats was exempt from any other agency oversight and retained sole authority to govern facilities under the Energy Reorganization Act of 1974. Distrust among agencies grew to the point that in 1989, the Federal Bureau of Investigation, Justice Department, and EPA launched a surprise raid, "Operation Desert Glow," to investigate allegations of environmental crimes. Hazardous conditions were apparent, and the federal government immediately shut down production at Rocky Flats while it decided how to best proceed.

According to a report of the General Accounting Office to Congress:

> The site's weapons production activities left high-risk radioactive and hazardous materials and wastes, severely contaminated buildings, and large areas of contaminated soil—all in close proximity to the 2.5 million residents of Denver and its surrounding communities. The job at hand is huge. For example, the total amount of radioactive waste that the contractor is required to package and ship off-site is enough to fill a 19-story building the size of a football field.[4]

Rocky Flats's 6,262-acre site had become one of the most dangerously contaminated locations in the world. The EPA placed Rocky Flats on the national priorities list and designated it as a Super Fund hazardous waste site. The official DOE 1995 Baseline Environmental Management Report estimated that the cleanup could take up to 75 years and cost up to $37 billion.[5] Other estimates ranged from $17 billion to $100 billion and from 65 years to 100 years.[6]

With a baseline estimate in hand, DOE hired Kaiser-Hill to manage the cleanup efforts. Kaiser-Hill tapped Nancy Tuor, who was well known for her political savvy and change management skills, to join the management team. Over the next ten years, Tuor would hold several roles at Kaiser-Hill, including that of CEO during the final two years of the cleanup effort. She knew the size of the job at hand: A total closure and cleanup of a nuclear production facility had never been accomplished anywhere in the world. Many deemed success to be improbable or even downright impossible.

But on October 13, 2005—just ten years after the baseline estimates were complete—clean became reality when DOE declared the site officially clean and closed. *National Geographic* magazine called Rocky Flats "DOE's poster child for cleanup success."[7] Even more impressive? The private industry/government collaboration came in a staggering $27 billion under initial baseline projections and 65 years ahead of schedule.[8]

But just how do they do it?

A 2005–2006 internal review of Microsoft's back-office procure-to-pay processes was sobering. Microsoft found it used 77,000 active suppliers and had 140 different systems to support its 96 subsidiaries. The Hackett Group—a benchmarking organization—ranked Microsoft in the bottom quartile in terms of process maturity. It found that valuable human resources were focused on nonstrategic activities, including spending 370,000 hours each year just producing reports.

A small team from Microsoft banded together to determine the best way to revamp the company's processes. Code-named OneFinance, the team initially spent a significant amount of time in whiteboard sessions strategizing how best to proceed. The conclusion? Create an outsourcing business model whereby the chosen service provider would have a Vested interest in Microsoft's long-term success. This would mean creating a true win-win approach; the future outsourcing partner would be highly compensated for helping Microsoft transform its back-office procure-to-pay processes.

Tim McBride, Microsoft's general manager for finance operations and former chief procurement officer, was on the original team. As the designated procurement representative, he knew what the team was up against: "Most procurement professionals are hard-wired to win. The problem is that Microsoft's conventional definition of winning means that if Microsoft wins, the supplier loses." Creating a true win-win mentality would mean changing how Microsoft perceived winning; both Microsoft and its provider would have to share in both the risk and the reward associated with the transformation efforts. Instead of thinking about What's In It For Me (WIIFMe), it was time to think about What's In It For We (WIIFWe).

But just how did Microsoft do it?

McDonald's has a secret sauce.

And it is not the one you are thinking of. It is all about how it treats its suppliers. Suppliers who sometimes invest years and millions of their own dollars to improve McDonald's products and processes, giving the company a huge competitive advantage in terms of a supply chain unparalleled in quality, safety, assured supply—*and* costs.

In the beginning there were suppliers such as J. R. Simplot, who perfected the frozen french fry and enabled McDonald's to serve fries made from the highest-quality Russet potatoes year-round. And Golden State Foods, which developed the famous "special sauce" for the Big Mac. And Jack Katz at Keystone Foods, who sunk millions of dollars in cryogenic freezing technologies to do what former McDonald's CEO Fred

Turner thought was impossible—create a frozen beef patty that was quicker and easier to prepare and was as juicy, and more tender, than a fresh patty. Cryogenically frozen beef made it possible for McDonald's to radically simplify its beef supply chain from hundreds of local suppliers to five core strategic suppliers, enabling the company to reduce costs and increase its already unequivocal demand for quality and safety.

Today, the legendary stories continue with U.S. supplier Danaco Solutions LLC, which has invested in fork-to-farm traceability, ensuring that McDonald's tomatoes are 100 percent traceable and free of salmonella and other harmful bacteria.

Danaco's Carey Cooper grew up in a family business that processed fresh vegetables, cutting up lettuce, tomatoes, and onions and packaging them for restaurants. Cooper knew the potential dangers of improperly handled produce first hand. "Produce is a dangerous product," he explained. "It's grown on the ground and subject to the same harmful pathogens to which meat is susceptible. However, produce isn't cooked and therefore can be more dangerous if tainted."

Cooper developed "a better way" to handle tomatoes— one of the most fragile of the produce items moving through McDonald's supply chain. He established strategic relationships with the three best-in-class growers and implemented improved safety processes and handling procedures.

When the Food and Drug Administration ordered a tomato recall in 2008, Danaco's solution was already in place. The Danaco team immediately traced the tomato supply chain and determined that McDonald's tomatoes were safe. Cooper related proudly, "Whether or not you have a tomato on your sandwich or salad may not be a crisis for you—but, as a McDonald's supplier, it is for Danaco and the growers we work with. All of McDonald's competitors had signs up for weeks that said 'out of tomatoes' or 'tomatoes available upon request only.' Not McDonald's."

It might not be a big deal to run out of tomatoes, but think about running out of chicken when you are in the chicken business. Suppliers made the difference during the avian flu crisis when competitors ran out of chicken—and McDonald's did not. McDonald's unequivocal fairness and focus on creating a tight alignment to its strategic Plan to Win makes the difference. And it is paying off. McDonald's is topping the charts on Wall Street and in *Forbes*, *Businessweek*, and virtually every other ranking.

But just how do McDonald's and its suppliers it?

VESTING FOR SUCCESS

This book is the biography of a business model, and the idea is very simple. We call it Vested. The premise? Create business relationships with experts outside of your domain to accomplish objectives so bold they have never been accomplished before. We call these relationships Vested because they involve creating a relationship (or relationships) in which the parties have a committed and profound interest in each other's success. Simply put, the parties are most successful when both are successful.

Vested thinking is different. It often means going against the grain in how suppliers and business partners traditionally approach working together. It requires long-term thinking, not short-term thinking. It is about working with suppliers as business partners rather than relying on tried-and-true procurement processes that use transactional buy-sell principles. It is about moving away from rigid contracts and statements of work and instead creating flexible business agreements based on trust, transparency, and fairness when business happens.

Some think it is a radical idea.

In pursuit of this radical idea, we are going to take you on the journey of how five organizations went against conventional wisdom and created long-term, deep business relationships based on trust, transparency, and—above all else—mutual success. Think of it as baking a bigger pie. One company is a chef and the other has ingredients. Together they create something neither party could do on its own. You might call it collaboration that works. Or win-win at its best. We call it Vested.

The organizations profiled in this book each took a step back and rethought how they could best achieve their goals—goals so lofty that no one had achieved them before. The stories we share reveal how the parties created business relationships yielding impressive results—results so successful the companies refer to them as transformational, game changing, and even award winning. Each of the stories reveals how the companies applied Vested principles to achieve their success.

We explore how P&G reached outside to bring innovation to the least suspecting corporate function: the mundane world of corporate facilities and real estate management. We share how powerhouses Microsoft and Accenture joined forces to drive radical improvements in back-office finance operations. We provide insights into how McDonald's and its suppliers have created a secret sauce for managing McDonald's vast supply chain operations.

But Vested thinking is not just for big companies. You will learn how the Minnesota Department of Transportation bridged the fallen highway and healed wounded hearts with the new I-35W Bridge. And we show how the Department of Energy and Kaiser-Hill literally turned a highly toxic site of weapons of mass destruction into a wildlife refuge—doing what many thought was impossible. We even share how the nonprofit group Water For People is applying Vesting principles in the quest to build partnerships and alliances to eliminate water poverty in developing countries.

The stories we share are transformational, and we hope they will inspire you to seek ways to develop your own hyperproductive business relationships. As you read the stories of P&G, Microsoft, McDonald's, the I-35W Bridge replacement, and Rocky Flats, challenge yourself to answer this question: Just how Vested am I in the success of my business partners? If you do not have a Vested interest in your business partners' success, then you are likely not getting the best from them.

2

P&G'S GAME CHANGER IN OUTSOURCING

Winning is pretty much the same in today's business world as it has been for decades. Create new customers, new products, and new services and drive revenue growth and profits. What's different is how to do it.

— A. G. Lafley, *former CEO of Procter & Gamble*

RULE #1: FOCUS ON OUTCOMES, NOT TRANSACTIONS

Adam Smith, an eccentric Scottish academician at Glasgow University, discussed the human propensity for self-interest and formulated the law of supply and demand in 1776 with the publication of *An Enquiry into the Nature and Causes of the Wealth of Nations*. Smith wrote that society benefits as a whole from a multiplicity of trading transactions because humans seek what is best for them, resulting in fairness and honesty among equals. As demand for repeat transactions emerged, trading preferences evolved, and modern transaction-based business models were born. These transaction-based business models have been the cornerstone of conventional business relationships ever since.

Transaction-based thinking focuses on negotiating agreements at a per-transaction level, either by paying for a business task (cost per item, cost per task) or on a cost-per-headcount basis. Unfortunately, many business professionals wrongly assume that a transaction-based business model is the most cost-efficient model. For simple transactions with abundant supply and low complexity, transaction-based business models likely are most efficient. Consider your typical dry-cleaning example, where transaction-based approaches work well. You take in your clothes and pay a cost per item. The more items you have, the higher your bill. It is simple, and it makes sense.

During the 1980s, businesses began to focus on using their power to improve their position in the marketplace. Strategic sourcing concepts and centralized procurement departments emerged to consolidate buying power. In 1983, Peter Kraljic introduced the Kraljic model, which analyzes the purchasing portfolio of a company with regard to profit impact and supply risk. It distinguishes among four product categories: leverage items, strategic items, noncritical items, and bottleneck items.

The Kraljic model was an instant hit. Kraljic's approach encouraged businesses to use their buying power to condition the supply chain and force change in the demand curve to lessen dependency on service providers. In short, it began a trend to encourage buyers to standardize and commoditize their suppliers. Strategic sourcing approaches also encouraged companies to decrease the number of suppliers they used and increase their use of competitive bids. Some companies took the concept to the extreme, having "every dollar, every year" procurement policies. Technology also emerged that enabled procurement groups to use reverse auction techniques that pitted suppliers against one other in an effort to help companies get the lowest possible price.

Unfortunately, the more companies flexed their procurement muscle, the more service providers hunkered down to protect their margins. These heavy-handed transaction-based approaches often led to perverse incentives and missed opportunities to innovate.[1] The weakness in transaction-based approaches emerges when the transaction includes any level of added complexity, variability, and mutual dependency. A transactional approach cannot produce perfect market-based price equilibrium in variable or multidimensional business agreements. You cannot simply switch out a husband or wife as easily as you can switch out your dry cleaner. The same is true when it comes to switching out suppliers that your company relies on—especially service-related suppliers, such as information technology (IT), call centers, or supply chain providers that play an integral part in delivering a company's solution.

Field-based research by the University of Tennessee shows that companies are challenging the conventional transaction-based approach for their most strategic business relationships and choosing to move to an outcome-based business model. P&G is one such company that is challenging the conventional approach.

P&G'S TRANSFORMATIONAL APPROACH FOR OUTSOURCING WITH JONES LANGE LASALLE

Procter & Gamble is known for changing the game to achieve a competitive advantage. P&G executives knew that for the company to continue to win, they needed to do what they did best: relentlessly apply a laser focus on the customer and P&G's commitment to innovation. As a result, in 1999 P&G executives decided to centralize 70+ non-core functions, such as IT, accounting and financial reporting, and facilities management/ workplace services into a newly organized Global Business Services (GBS) group.[2]

By 2002, P&G executives knew GBS could take the company only so far with efficiencies and began to explore outsourcing. In 2003, Filippo Passerini was asked to take the helm of P&G's GBS organization and lead the company's transformation efforts.

One area that was suitable for transformation was facilities management.

Over the years, P&G had built, leased, or inherited facilities on a country-by-country basis on five continents. It occupied 150+ office and research facilities spanning more than 17 million square feet in 86 countries. An in-house crew of about 550 people provided services for the buildings. In addition, for nearly 20 years some of the hourly work, such as cleaning, had been contracted out locally. The hodgepodge of community and regional contractors met local needs, but the overall approach to facilities management fell far short of a coordinated, global strategy. Duplication across regions proliferated in procurement, hiring, and oversight. Due to the variability of processes across countries, it was difficult to drive effective and efficient global controls and a compliance environment. One thing that P&G's executives always wanted was to have facilities management data collected and reported on a global basis. Gaining ready access to worldwide results and trends put transformation on the fast track.

Passerini knew that if he was to be successful, he needed to motivate his team to develop innovative approaches to drive transformational productivity results. He recalled the time he spent in P&G line management. He could not remember any "or" options. The pressure was for higher profit *and* higher market share, better quality *and* lower costs. Passerini knew that to drive innovation in GBS, his team needed to think in terms of AND, not OR. "We brought this mind-set to shared services," Passerini said "It's and, and, and, and."[3] To this day, within the P&G environment the "Power of AND" remains a guiding principle.

"The time was ripe for making the move to outsource," explained Passerini. "Our objective was to further cut costs *and* improve service levels. By outsourcing the more repetitive commodity work and keeping in-house what we considered strategic, we could, in effect, enable ourselves to focus on innovation and developing new business capabilities for P&G."[4]

Passerini's leadership inspired confidence that the business was on track for renewed profitability and shareholder satisfaction. However, employees within the GBS group became restless and apprehensive about their futures.[5] Consistent with long-held company values, Passerini opted to communicate with employees within an "adult business relationship," respecting employees with the intent to maintain a high level of transparency and keep employees up to date. In addition, P&G developed processes that gave employees a seat at the decision-making table, allowing employees from all ranks of P&G to help design how the company approached outsourcing.

Last, P&G committed to protect employees' jobs. Whatever decision was made, P&G employees would not be labeled "redundant." They would not lose their jobs as a result of the outsourcing efforts.

Moving from concept to action, P&G recruited William Reeves, an Alabama native who had been with the company for more than 30 years, to lead the outsourcing efforts of facilities management services for the GBS organization.

THE JOURNEY BEGINS

P&G began its outsourcing journey by searching for a facilities management service provider that could help P&G move into the twenty-first century with greatly improved cost structures and services. Reeves had spent his first 21 years in a pure IT career path but expanded his career as P&G's GBS organization evolved. As the company moved to a shared-services environment, his engagement with other workplace services grew. Reeves, a black belt in Tae Kwon Do, loves a good challenge and set out to make Passerini's challenge a reality.

Reeves started by questioning conventional approaches to outsourcing. He knew if he and his fellow P&Gers were to succeed, they would have to solve a common paradox in strategic outsourcing. That is, how could P&G outsource its current facilities management processes and, at the same time, transform its properties to be more effective and efficient? What motivation would there be for potential suppliers to make substantial efficiency gains while using current processes and people? After all, more transactions and headcount traditionally mean more revenue for the service provider.

Reeves needed to be creative. A reinvention of the approach to facilities management potentially could save P&G a great deal of money, generate efficiencies and process standardization, and enable resources to focus on key priorities. But to fully realize the promise, the approach had to be effective long term. Reeves needed to create an outsourcing solution based on a system that would be accountable and reliable for years to come.

The solution was to flip the conventional outsourcing approach on its head: P&G would focus much of its efforts on contracting for *transformation* instead of contracting for day-to-day work. Reeves no longer wanted P&G employees and vendors to simply take *care* of their buildings; he wanted to develop an outsourcing relationship in which the future P&G service provider took *charge* of the buildings.

A radical idea.

OUTCOMES, NOT TRANSACTIONS

Focusing on outcomes and not transactions is a big test for any company, P&G included. "This was a big cultural change," Passerini explained. "However, when we talk of cultural changes, we must keep in mind that we can't commandeer culture. It is the product of organizational design, of building skills and competencies, and of rewarding people when they do well. My own leadership philosophy is about launching breakthrough ideas and setting goals. It's about starting with the end in mind and forcing a pace to deliver on the goals. It is about creating support systems that enable the organization to perform, to feel motivated and good about itself. It's about raising the energy level."[6]

The challenge Reeves faced was to create the right synergies that would shift the energy P&G invested in daily activities to the more critical area of top-line growth. Outsourcing non-core facilities management functions such as maintenance, security, space planning, and cafeteria management was an integral part of his overall plan.

Reeve's team members spent a significant amount of time determining what outcomes they wanted to achieve. While cutting costs was important, P&G really wanted to create world-class processes and an infrastructure that would serve the company as it continued to grow. The P&G/JLL team developed these desired outcomes:

- Provide services of equal or better quality at a lower cost.
- Enjoy world-class supplier support, dedicated account management.
- Build a global relationship to support P&G business objectives.
- Have a supplier that guarantees the availability of resources.
- Allow P&G to satisfy the facilities management needs of a world-class global corporation.[7]

A key P&G strategy was to establish a commercial agreement based on holding the potential service provider accountable for achieving results. The approach would require service providers to continuously bring new ideas and determine the best way to get results.

P&Gers like to think of the outcome-based approach to alignment as pulling on a rope in the same direction. The traditional approach is to have a buyer and supplier on each end of a rope, with each party trying to hold its position as they negotiate. The P&G way of thinking is to have suppliers on the same side of the rope, with both parties pulling in the same direction to achieve cost and service objectives. Doing so results in more power to drive transformation and embrace the dynamic changes that the business world throws P&G's way.

LAYING THE FOUNDATION: GETTING TO WE

Once P&G envisioned the model, it explored the possibilities through a request for proposal process aimed at market leaders who could transform its facilities management worldwide.

When the potential list was narrowed to a handful of respondents P&G added a unique next step to gain critical insight into the potential supplier's competency. Suppliers were asked to conduct three-day site visits at five locations around the world to study the sites, understand the P&G business, and develop a five-year action plan describing how they would manage the business.

Jones Lange LaSalle (JLL) took P&G's challenge seriously as it prepared its application. JLL's chief financial officer (CFO) and chief operating officer (COO) Lauralee Martin reflected, "P&G set out saying they wanted a global, unified relationship, something JLL had not done previously with any client. JLL needed to rise to the occasion and rethink how to deliver on this deal. Right from the beginning—this was strategically important to both of us—beyond the deal itself. To be successful, both companies knew each company would need to respect each other's capabilities. The discussions were around how 1 + 1 would equal far more than 2 by having the companies work together. JLL made a strategic decision to invest in getting to really understand P&G's business and to think creatively about ways to bring process innovation to P&G."[8]

Based on the proposals submitted, P&G could tell who had invested the time and had the potential skills. Reeves explained, "Some suppliers have good chase teams for sales but not operations. Our process gave us a lens to see beyond a supplier's sales team. The five-year action plans each of the suppliers created allowed us to see who really understood our business and the challenges we faced. We had already streamlined significantly, and to get to the next level we required true transformation. It was easy to see which suppliers did deep dives based on how insightful their observations were. The supplier reports showed they could manage our processes in a better way—something that was key for P&G."[9]

In the end, the P&G team decided to move forward with JLL, and Reeves was pleased with the selection. He had noticed during meetings that there were no discernible culture differences when JLL and P&G folks met; it was hard to tell who worked for which company. Cultural compatibility is an important element of successful Vested partnerships. Reeves reported: "JLL was a good fit. Both companies had impressive histories and records of performance excellence, but P&G and JLL shared something even more important—similar corporate ethics and commitments."[10]

The public statements on each company's web site evidence the compatibility of corporate cultures. Figure 2.1 provides a few examples.

Reeves summed up the relationship when he met with Bill Thummel, the JLL global account executive, to let him know about P&G's decision. Thummel was Reeves's counterpart for JLL's facilities management operation. Reeves shook hands with

Figure 2.1 Comparison of P&G and Jones Lang LaSalle Corporate Cultures

Stated Principle/ Value Category	P&G	Jones Lang LaSalle
Workplace	We attract and recruit the finest people in the world. We build our organization from within, promoting and rewarding people without regard to any difference unrelated to performance.	We strive to attract and retain the most talented individuals, encouraging and enabling them to succeed. We foster an inclusive environment that values the richness of our differences and reflects the diverse world in which we work
Community	P&G and its employees have a long-standing commitment to being good citizens and neighbors in all the places where we do business around the world.	We endeavor to be good citizens wherever we live and work.
Ethics and Corporate Governance	P&G has been built through the character of its people. That character is reflected in the Company's Values, which have been fundamental to our success for more than 175 years. Our continued success depends on each one of us doing our part to uphold these values in our day-to-day work and in all the decisions we make.	We are proud of our global reputation for uncompromising integrity, ethical conduct and corporate governance. Our Code of Business Ethics and Vendor Code of Conduct are followed by our own employees and everyone who does business on behalf of our firm. We are also proud of the rigor and quality of the firm's corporate governance and the benefits these policies produce for our stakeholders.

Thummel to symbolically seal the deal, stating, "We know that you [JLL] and the other suppliers we evaluated have never done this before; and neither have we. But JLL has the culture that is much like P&G's. We think we have the best chance of being successful with you because you are so much like us."

The trust implied within a handshake is taken seriously at P&G. Known for its ethical business practices, P&G actually built a conference room in the executive building called the "Handshake Room." That is not a nickname—"Handshake Room" is etched on the door, lest people forget why they are meeting there. It is a small room with two video screens and a dozen seats where leaders gather to discuss potential collaborative projects; if the project's a go, executives shake on it and agree on how to charge ahead.

In essence, Reeves and Thummel set the tone of the relationship that day. Based on their handshake, P&G vowed to respect and honor JLL's role as P&G's expert in facilities management, and JLL accepted responsibility to jointly move into uncharted territory.

The P&G/JLL outsourcing effort was the largest facilities outsourcing deal in history. The contract, signed in June 2003, was groundbreaking due to its global scope (covering 60 countries) and multidisciplinary nature (facility management, project management, and strategic occupancy services). The controllable operating expenses for these services were estimated at $700 million over five years and initially spanned about 14 million square feet. From a facilities management standpoint, this was the largest relationship that P&G had established with a single supplier. JLL's Martin recalled the focus both companies put on the relationship and getting the deal right. "Right from the start the relationship enjoyed recognition, support, and drive from both P&G and JLL. It took courage. The focus, the objectives, it was a partnership. We kept this high-level connection all the way through."

Starting with values and moving through day-to-day operations, P&G and JLL set out to create a winning partnership to deliver results, not just people to perform facilities management tasks.

Of course, both companies were used to focusing on results. Each had a long history of delivering results that added real business value to its bottom line. But the P&G and JLL relationship had a new twist. Both companies understood that winning needed to be a shared experience. Creating a true win-win mentality meant changing the rules of the game; both P&G and JLL would share in the risk and reward associated with the transformation efforts. Instead of thinking about "What's In It For Me" (WIIFMe), it was time to think about "What's In It For We" (WIIFWe).

One example of this is how P&G and JLL respected existing employees. In outsourcing tradition, existing employees typically are laid off and replaced with less expensive workers in a practice called labor arbitrage.

P&G approached the situation differently. It is a promote-from-within company, and many of its employees had spent years—if not their entire careers—at the firm. P&G refused to turn its back on loyal employees. Workers were advised at the beginning of the process that they would not be laid off; their jobs would be transferred to whatever outsource provider was chosen.

Reeves explained, "P&G's own people became our service providers' employees, delivering the same services." The contract basically transferred all current practice, including vendors and P&G employees, to JLL with the starting point to keep things "as is, where is." Although the P&Gers would be rebadged to become employees of JLL, their day-to-day work would stay the same.

JLL also came out a winner in this approach. P&G had a loyal and trained worldwide workforce. JLL did not physically have employees in many of the countries in which P&G operated, such as Egypt and Greece. The agreement immediately expanded JLL's global footprint. In addition, transferring existing P&G employees made for an easier transition. By January 2004, about 550 P&G employees were rebadged, and the partnership took off.[11]

Like many other P&G leaders, Tim McParlane accepted a position with JLL. McParlane was the senior point person for GBS outsourcing in North America at the time P&G was exploring potential service providers. As the decision-making process moved forward, McParlane considered his own future. He decided that moving to JLL would allow him to grow his career in real estate management. McParlane said, "I felt very comfortable that JLL was a company with a culture similar to P&G. I knew working for JLL would not only be a good place to work, but that I had a formal career ladder in my chosen field, the professional real estate industry."

And getting off to a good start in the new career is exactly what McParlane and his JLL counterparts did. Passerini was indeed pleased. "I asked our internal business partners—P&G's operating units—if they knew what day we transferred many of our services to our outsourcing partner. They hadn't even noticed it happen. So for them it was mainly a change of badge."[12]

Shifting work—often referred to as lift-and-shift strategy— was just the starting point for the P&G/JLL relationship. With a successful global transition under their belts, P&G and JLL knew it was time to focus on the real reason why P&G out-sourced—to achieve the Power of AND. P&G made it clear that JLL was accountable for delivering service that greatly reduced P&G's costs *and* for creating initiatives that would deliver real business value. Simply put, P&G bought transformation.

LEADING A PARADIGM SHIFT

As the senior most JLL executive for the P&G account, Thummel worried that many former P&Gers would fall victim to the junk-yard dog syndrome. This is when outsourced employees hunker down and resist change because "they've always done the job this way." This was a real risk because rebadged employees performed the same kind of work they used to—only now as JLL employees.

Although daily work remained unchanged, Thummel immediately began to educate former P&Gers that being JLL employees was a fundamental change. The goal was that all JLL employees would learn to align their daily decisions and actions to the contract provisions instead of automatic past practice. Could they streamline processes? How could they positively impact P&G's sustainability efforts? Were they taking enough time on preventive equipment maintenance to reduce downtime? "Employees needed to learn how to be JLL employees and accept responsibility to drive innovations in jobs where they had worked for years," explained Thummel.

Simply put, the former P&Gers would need to challenge the status quo on a daily basis if JLL was to meet its contractual commitments. For that reason, Thummel required managers to study the contract, which represented JLL's commitments to P&G and what delivering against those commitments meant. It also represented how JLL made money. For the first few months, JLL meetings started with reading and discussing portions of the contract to help the top managers (including former P&Gers) understand the importance of the overall goals. The team jokingly referred to this exercise as "the daily prayer sessions." They started by picking areas they knew would be difficult or potentially contentious. In addition, McParlane developed written tests to verify that the entire JLL team understood the contract. What set the contract apart was that it was flexible and dealt with dynamic changes that might arise in the course of business. Any business professional will tell you "business happens." It is important to stay flexible and position your company to take advantage of the dynamic nature of business—both the upside and the downside.

Former P&Gers realized they now worked for a company where real estate and facilities management *was* the business.

As JLL employees, they did not simply hold support positions; they gained formal career ladders as real estate professionals. For example, McParlane now holds a regional director position within JLL. In fact, many of the original transferred employees have been promoted, some within the P&G account and some for other clients. As time passed, employee satisfaction increased as the work became more rewarding and more challenging.

Reeves, who keeps track of fellow P&G employees, said, "It's one of the things I'm most proud about. We went through a process and found the right firm for a long-term relationship. It works and continues to work for the employees."

FROM TRANSITION TO TRANSFORMATION

All too often in an outsourcing agreement, it is easy to fall into what is commonly referred to as the Activity Trap: delivering just against the day-to-day tasks while failing to deliver on the overall end objectives of why a company outsourced in the first place. "We had to keep in mind P&G bought transformation, not just workers to do the job. If we simply...performed work the way it had been done, JLL would fail," explained Thummel.

Early on—within the first four months—JLL identified every single commitment made in the contract. Thummel and his team spent three entire days going through and condensing the list to create a project plan. Referred to as the "Transformation Plan," it provided clarity for priorities, phases, and time lines. Thummel explained the power of this approach: "Showing P&G the plan distilled transformation into something that was doable and had a time line associated with it. It was all clear. And, most importantly, it helped both P&G and JLL see the end game." The plan brought another important benefit, according to Thummel. "This really helped us ensure P&G did not get frustrated with

JLL because we were not delivering everything all at once. It set the tone that achieving results relied on an orderly process of taking good ideas and turning them into initiatives that generate real benefits once implemented."

By then, Reeves and Thummel had established a solid working relationship. In a typical friendly conversation, Thummel assured Reeves, "We will share this transformation plan again in four years and show you we delivered on our commitments, and you will have no doubt you made the right decision for a partner and will renew our contract."

The approach became known as the Glidepath because, as results were generated, P&G expected to see GBS cost as a percentage of sales graphed out in a downward-sloping line depicting lower costs over time—in essence, costs would glide down.

One of the key initiatives JLL brought to P&G was known as Bundled Soft Services, the term for an initiative to "bundle" the scope of work. Traditionally, separate suppliers provided services such as cleaning, mail, package delivery, and meeting arrangements. Common sense says economies happen as cross-training/multirole hiring occurs. If people were hired to sort and deliver external mail, it made sense that they also could sort and deliver internal communications, flowers, and the like. Bundling enabled JLL to consolidate and reduce administrative expenses. The idea was simple: JLL would replace multiple soft services contracts with a vastly reduced number of second-tier vendor contracts. The problem was how to implement this key concept.

McParlane had wanted to institute bundling when he was a P&G employee, but he just could not get traction for it. The concept had never been implemented before in the facilities management industry. P&G felt it was too risky and did not want to devote the required resources to the project. McParlane and his JLL colleagues were confident that the timing was perfect.

The challenge of transforming P&G's operation was exciting. The Bundled Soft Services idea and over a hundred others formed the basis of a detailed matrix that measured customer impact, difficulty, and time for implementation for each idea.

But a few months into the contract, JLL ran into one of its first roadblocks. It happened when senior managers from both companies worldwide met at P&G headquarters to go over the list of ideas and proposed initiatives. During the joint leadership meeting, the two companies bandied about various initiatives, but no decisions were made. A couple of hours in, JLL team members were getting frustrated; the P&G leadership team was not signing off on the initiatives. The clock was ticking down; the longer it took to implement new ideas, the fewer the savings and the less likelihood the companies would achieve the Glidepath objectives. There was what one might call "healthy tension" in the room. When the topic of Bundled Software Solutions came up, various P&G employees stated versions of "Oh, we've thought of that before...it will be too hard to do!"

Thummel stood and spoke out. Commanding attention, but with a grin, he said, "You say you want innovation, but you won't accept change!" He was chuckling because he knew Reeves would agree.

P&G's Reeves instantly stood and offered a direct, simple response. "You are right. And that is precisely what we do not want to do." Most folks in the room started laughing; they all realized Reeves and Thummel were right. The tone of the meeting immediately changed, and the joint team began to make progress. That day the Bundled Soft Services and dozens of other initiatives were approved.

JLL went on to implement the Bundled Soft Services initiative, which proved to be a winner. In the Middle East and Africa region alone, the simplified supply chain delivered a 60 percent reduction in service contracts and an overall supply base reduction of 45 percent. This kind of initiative helped JLL drive new cost reductions totaling 20 percent within the first five years of taking over P&G's facilities management operations.

TRANSFORMATION: BEYOND COST SAVINGS

A fundamental reason why P&G outsourced was to achieve transformation. Perhaps no better example shows how it and JLL work together to transform and drive value for P&G business and customers than their work in environmental sustainability. When P&G and JLL set out to renew their contract in 2007, both wanted to make a meaningful difference in the area of environmental sustainability. P&G hoped to aggressively shrink energy use and resource waste throughout its entire supply chain. And it wanted JLL's help.

JLL embraced the same goal of global environmental sustainability. "JLL was excited about the challenge for much the same reason as P&G was," explained Colin Dyer, JLL's chief executive officer. "JLL is the leading global real estate services and investment management company. Buildings typically contribute 40 percent of a country's total CO_2 emissions. Amid growing concern about rising greenhouse gas emissions, JLL accepts responsibility—and welcomes the opportunity—to contribute to solving this worldwide challenge with P&G." The philosophy was—and still is—that together P&G and JLL can combine their collective skill sets and tackle this "wicked problem."

CFO/COO Lauralee Martin summed up JLL's philosophy: "When we made our commitment to sustainability, we embedded real talent in this area. If you are just going to look at something from...the cost perspective [energy reduction], you miss the whole value chain [driving culture change]." Shared values matter.

JLL assigned Cindy Hill, VP Global Sustainability Manager, to join P&G's first Site Sustainability team. The team's goal was to create a tool kit for the P&G corporate sustainability initiative.

The working group included personnel from the P&G Research and Development Group, GBS, and JLL. Together, they tackled how to reduce P&G's environmental footprint measured in energy use, water use, and waste reduction.

In her new role, Hill led the JLL site facility team to harvest the "low-hanging fruit" by documenting energy use, studying behavior, and coming up with ways to impact workplace performance. Ultimately, the Green Office Tool Kit was developed; it explained the types of people to enlist on the team, what areas to look at, how to do it cost effectively, and how to engage employees. To deploy P&G's green initiatives to the rest of the JLL-managed facilities around the world, Hill became the first JLL resource on the P&G account dedicated solely to environmental sustainability.

Impacting environmental sustainability as a facilities management supplier is a tricky concept. How much can be quantifiably changed? For measurement purposes, how can you factor in older research buildings that require two to five times the energy of an office building? Is it fair to hold JLL accountable for results that depend on cooperation of individual P&G employees? "After all," Hill thought, "we can put recycling bins in every corner, but we can't force people to drop in their cans and paper."

JLL works with dedicated P&G teams at each location that are responsible for energy, water, and waste reductions as well as for deploying P&G Earth Day programs to raise employee awareness of corporate sustainability objectives. In addition, sustainability criteria are part of any future space assessment to ensure that new locations align with corporate goals.

Working together, P&G and JLL created a partnership culture. A key to their success is something P&G and JLL call the "2 in a Box" concept. P&G and JLL leaders devise strategies to meet P&G's desired outcomes. Hill's 2 in a Box partner is Larry Bridge, and together they aim to educate employees and influence more sustainable workplace behaviors to meet P&G's energy goals by using three primary strategies.[13]

1. They promote energy reduction through remodeling improvements—new boilers, better windows, more efficient lighting, and the like.
2. They tighten processes and procedures for efficiency (i.e., managing hours of operation, installing smart printers and motion-controlled lighting).
3. They facilitate employee education and behavior modification.

A great example of how the two companies work together is their approach to sustainability awareness programs. P&G uses an e-training tool developed by JLL as inspiration to create P&G-specific training available to all employees. JLL works with the GBS organization to use P&G branding strategies to encourage employee engagement in recycling and saving paper waste with reusable tumblers in cafeterias, etc.

Since JLL and P&G joined forces for facility management, global P&G energy consumption has fallen 14 percent. Decision makers consider environmental sustainability in every capital investment, renovation, and space reutilization. And, just as important, when the low-hanging fruit is long gone, the incremental, sustainable savings will add up to long-term results.

On a micro scale, P&G's 1.5 million-square-foot headquarters in Cincinnati received an Energy Star label in February 2007, becoming one of the largest of the 650 private-sector office properties to gain the rating distinction. This was a direct result of P&G and JLL working together.

VESTED FOR SUCCESS

After eight years, the P&G/JLL deal has proven that it is possible to develop a true win-win partnership. JLL proved it could balance what some would call a paradox—achieving high service levels *and* reducing costs. P&G proved it could truly outsource work for the betterment of both companies.

Larry Bridge, the P&G leader in charge of contract governance, put it this way: "As much as we give credit to relationships, we have a really good contract. It is simple and drives the right behaviors. Transparency, cost pass-through, and incentives features allow us to be aligned versus being on opposites sides of the table negotiating."[14]

P&G and JLL have a true Vested business relationship in which everyone is a winner. JLL not only met expected cost savings objectives, it achieved the savings without sacrificing customer satisfaction. P&G's "customers"—the employees who use the facilities—are JLL's real customers. JLL has exceeded the satisfaction target for six consecutive years. In addition, JLL emphasized the use of minority suppliers for secondary outsourcing contracts, helping P&G exceed its minority supplier spend goal for six consecutive years.

Ask any JLL team member and he or she will tell you that JLL wins as well. Incentive pay structured into the contract is highly motivating for JLL, but equally important is the opportunity to earn more business. In 2007, P&G decided to renew its contract with JLL early. In 2008, P&G awarded JLL the real estate services contract for the entire P&G portfolio. Earning the second contract gave JLL the opportunity to provide even more strategic value.

With the early renewal of the original agreement and the addition of real estate services, both parties were confident that their relationship could reach even greater heights.

Lauralee Martin—JLL's COO and CFO—felt confident that JLL could continue to see results from the innovation efforts. She said, "Many service providers are hesitant to step up and commit to continue to guarantee improvements year over year. We find the opposite is true. It's often actually easier to deliver results when the basis is from innovation and not simply cost cutting. That is because results from innovation are like an evolving story. You find savings in one area and it unlocks the door to another. If you want to get to the ultimate end game, you leverage on previous innovations."

P&G's Reeves has a similar philosophy. He believes that innovation has the same principles that he knew growing up in the farm fields in Alabama. Reeves has been heard to say, "You plant seeds, and you wait for them to come up. Then you cultivate them and do what needs to be done to help them grow."[15]

The P&G/JLL relationship has been a huge success, but P&G is quick to point out that it does not think it is an anomaly. P&G has taken what it has learned and scaled it to other suppliers—a model few other companies can claim.

Passerini and his team rose to A. G. Lafley's challenge. GBS's results are real—and quantifiable:

- Reduced GBS cost as a percentage of sales by 33 percent
- Service levels up 17 points (from 80 to 97)
- Speed to market two times faster
- Delivering 75 percent more service scope than seven years ago
- Managing three times the number of complex initiatives
- Acquisitions and divestitures time cut in half
- *And* more capacity to innovate[16]

"This kind of achievement can only be achieved by challenging the status quo and bringing innovation—the Power of the AND," explains Lydia Jacobs-Horton, P&G GBS Director, Global Facilities and Real Estate. "We expect our suppliers to bring innovative ideas to help us with our toughest problems, and that is exactly what JLL has done."[17]

Today, P&G's GBS organization has been recognized externally as the best shared-services organization in the world—with Passerini receiving *InformationWeek*'s Chief of the Year recognition and being inducted into the CIO Hall of Fame in

2010. Internally, GBS has dramatically improved in the annual P&G company employee satisfaction survey, moving from last place a few years ago to the top spot for two years running. The P&G web site sums it up nicely:

> P&G's Global Business Services (GBS) extends and multiplies the company's abilities by streamlining operations, accelerating internal collaboration, and by scaling systems, services, and processes globally. The GBS organization has been in operation for more than 10 years and has provided the company a competitive advantage through new business models, unique partner relationships and distinctive strategies.

MINNESOTA TURNS I-35W BRIDGE TRAGEDY INTO TRIUMPH

> The significant problems we face cannot be solved at the same
> level of thinking we were at when we created them.
>
> —*Albert Einstein*

RULE #2: FOCUS ON THE *WHAT*, NOT THE *HOW*

IS THERE A BETTER WAY?

Is there a better way? Perhaps no other question encapsulates the drive for innovation permeating today's business environment. It is what drove Albert Einstein and Thomas Edison to challenge the status quo to create not just better products but also better solutions. It is what drives business people to solve complex problems to meet customer needs.

Finding a better way is what challenges the telecommunications industry to continuously reinvent itself, shifting from wall-mounted crank phones to desktop dial models to touch tone to wireless and now sleek, portable cell phones that include a full-fledged computer, video camera, audio/video playback, and high-speed Internet access. Finding a better way is not just a quandary for inventors, technologists, and engineers. It is what smart companies ask their employees, suppliers, and business partners to consider as they strive to continually improve their products and services.

Why is innovation such a challenge at most organizations?

In today's world, no organization functions alone. All major organizations require business partners to get things done. And frequently those relationships impede innovative ideas rather than foster them. After researching dozens of supplier relationships, we began to see a common theme emerge. Simply put, companies actually tend to get what they ask for and what they pay for. The problem is that what they ask for and pay for is not necessarily what they really want. Let us look at what we call the outsourcing paradox.

We found a classic example of the paradox at work in a third-party logistics provider that runs a spare parts warehouse. During a site visit, we saw approximately eight people servicing a facility that averaged less than 75 orders per day. We asked, "Why all the resources?" The logistics provider replied, "The customer specifies staffing levels within our statement of work, so we schedule that many people in order to meet the contract requirements."

We see companies fall into a trap of trying to tightly define the "perfect" set of tasks, frequencies, and measures for suppliers. Their goal is to create excruciatingly precise requirements. After all, experts tell us that we need to clearly specify expectations, right? The result is an impressive document containing every possible detail about *how* the work is to be done. However, this "perfect system" is often the first reason that a company fails to get the innovation it seeks. That is because it is the *company's* perfect system, not one designed by the service provider. We call this the *outsourcing paradox* because the company outsources to the experts and then tells them how to do the work. In short, they get what they ask for.

We have seen statements of work that are 800 pages long and contain over 500 metrics. On a recent conference call, one vice president discussed the 2,400-page contract, which he was in charge of and which he had not read. Such overly prescriptive documents virtually tie suppliers' hands, forcing them to think *inside* the box rather than bring creative solutions to solve business problems or optimize for efficiencies. The very length of the comprehensive document limits a supplier's ability to bring real value.

An ill-written, task-frequency specification contract can create a harmful and insurmountable barrier to innovation. After all, how can suppliers innovate when they are contractually required to do the work a certain, predetermined way?

Our research has shown that progressive organizations challenge the conventional wisdom of heavily prescribing how to do the work. Instead, they shift their effort—to focus on the *what* versus prescribing the *how*. This rest of this chapter focuses on the story of how the Minnesota Department of Transportation (MnDOT) resisted the urge to tell potential construction contractors how to design and build the I-35W replacement bridge.

THE BATTLE WITH THE BRIDGE

August 1, 2007.

The world held its collective breath during rush hour as Minnesota's Bridge #9340 buckled and then collapsed into the Mississippi River. One hundred and eleven vehicles were traveling across the I-35W Bridge as it tumbled 64 feet into the muddy water, submerging 17 cars and stranding many others. A damaged semitrailer caught fire, as did several cars. A school bus carrying 63 children perched precariously against a guardrail; Jeremy Hernandez, a 20-year-old staff member, kicked open the back emergency exit and helped the students to exit safely. In the end, 13 people lost their lives and 145 suffered injuries as a result of the bridge collapse.

Unfortunately, it should have come as no surprise.

Opened in 1967, the 1,907-foot-long truss arch bridge complied with the 1961 "Standard Specifications for Highway Bridges" of the American Association of State Highway Officials.[1] Bridge #9340 was a vital part of the U.S. Interstate System, I-35W, and the Minneapolis community. Its eight lanes carried 140,000 vehicles daily. The architects, Sverdrup and Parcel, anticipated the bridge's lifetime to be 50 years. Unfortunately, it took only 23 years for signs of corrosion of bearings and fatigue cracks in bridge approach spans to signal significant problems.

In 1990, the U.S. Department of Transportation classified Bridge #9340 as "structurally deficient." This rating was repeated each year until 2007, when the bridge collapsed.[2] Internal MnDOT communications referred to just such a possibility and worried that it might have to be condemned.

In 2007, the bridge was four years from the end of its expected life, and warning signs of a potential failure were everywhere. A meeting between URS Corporation, an engineering and consulting firm, and MnDOT was scheduled for August 20, 2007, to determine how best to proceed. The meeting never happened. The bridge collapsed 19 days before the scheduled meeting.

MnDOT had not been complacent about the reported conditions. It had battled with bridge deficiencies for years. In fact, the bridge was undergoing repair when it collapsed. Construction had closed four of the eight lanes, and 575,000 pounds of construction supplies and equipment were on the bridge. The bridge's gussets—thick steel plates that connect beams to one another—could not bear the load, and the center span separated and fell into the water. Ultimately, the National Transportation Safety Board ruled that the primary reason for Bridge #9340's collapse was improperly designed gussets. Historically, industry experts presumed gussets to be stronger than the members they connect; typically gussets were not tested as part of load ratings.

The bridge's failure caused not only tragic loss of life; the loss of one of the major traffic arteries in the Twin Cities area had dire monetary consequences. Experts estimated that the collapsed bridge cost the community in excess of $1 million a day. The MnDOT Office of Investment Management estimated the daily cost to motorists to be $400,000. The State Department of Economic Development believed that the bridge failure would have an average negative net economic impact of $113,000 daily on the state's economic output. And the Minneapolis Regional Chamber of Commerce estimated that the daily cost to business exceeded $500,000.

The magnitude of impact could not be determined exactly, but everyone agreed that delay was not an option. MnDOT needed to build a new bridge. Quickly. Minnesota governor Tim Pawlenty challenged the department to complete a replacement bridge within 18 months. Considering that it typically takes that long (or longer) just to identify the scope of a project of this size, MnDOT knew it needed to approach this rebuild in a very different way.

A radical approach led to a radical result. The new, state-of-the-art I-35W St. Anthony Falls Bridge opened for business on September 18, 2008—one year and 17 days after the collapse. Cars lined up for hours for the privilege of following first responders, state troopers, and MnDOT construction vehicles at 5:00 A.M. for the official first crossing. The bridge is a breathtaking piece of architecture and technology that has won over 20 awards, including being named the 2009 Grand Prize winner of America's Transportation Awards for "representing the best in innovative management, accountability and timeliness."

The rest of this chapter focuses on how MnDOT and its team of suppliers turned tragedy into triumph.

TURNING TRAGEDY INTO TRIUMPH

The bridge collapse devastated MnDOT's project manager (PM), Jon Chiglo. "Of course, I took it personally. Everybody in the department took it personally. Lifetime careers had been built on designing structures that are sustainable and safe. There was an enormous amount of pride. It was just a nightmare for anybody to go through this. It was something you had to take personally."[3]

The nature of the tragedy demanded sensitivity as well as haste; conflicting feelings of fear and guilt, and a gut determination to make it right, demanded something other than business as usual.

MnDOT moved nimbly to meet the challenge. Within 18 hours of the bridge collapse, representatives of the City of Minneapolis, the Federal Highway Administration, and MnDOT met to decide how to begin rebuilding. They enlisted the help of transportation industry leader Tom Warren, who happened to be in town collaborating on another project. Chiglo, one of three MnDOT PMs who attended the gathering, received the project manager post that afternoon—less than 24 hours after the collapse.

Chiglo knew that rebuilding the I-35W Bridge required a profoundly different approach from standard MnDOT procurement processes, under which it could take as long as five years before construction would even begin. Clearly, this was unacceptable. In order for the project to meet the aggressive schedule, as well as limitations of funding, the rules needed an upgrade.

The MnDOT procurement model generally used a cost-plus, low-bid approach for contracting. These contracts provide payment of allowable incurred costs to suppliers to establish an estimate of total cost for the purpose of obligating funds and a ceiling that contractors may not exceed (except at their own risk) without the approval of the contracting officer. Both politicians and MnDOT officials also believed it was logical to use the traditional low-bid method of procurement in order to prevent abuse in the award of public projects.

The cost-plus, low-bid model is an approach paved with the good intentions of watching out for taxpayer dollars. However, Chiglo knew that the cost-plus, low-bid approach has fundamental flaws. For one thing, cost and time overruns are common. Contractors have little incentive to innovate or bring expenses down; doing so may actually reduce their profits.

Chiglo and the team immediately began to investigate more progressive approaches. At the top of the list was Minnesota Statute 161.3410, a law passed in 2001 that authorized MnDOT, Minnesota state colleges and universities, and the University of Minnesota to use alternative procurement methods.

The 2001 law was a paradigm shift that challenged government procurement agencies to stop seeing "low bid" as the obvious answer and instead consider "best value." The new law infused discretion back into the process. In passing the bill, the legislature demonstrated its belief that in certain circumstances a different delivery system could achieve better results.

Chiglo's team quickly decided to use the best value approach. Their rationale? It enabled them to balance cost, quality, and timeliness as key factors in how they chose the contractors ultimately responsible for rebuilding the bridge.

The team knew that the law also opened another door. Specifically, it granted permission for a design-build procurement model, also known as construction management at risk. Traditionally, MnDOT used a design-bid-build delivery method. This meant MnDOT designed the project, either internally or with consultants, and then put the plans and specifications out for bidding. Usually, quantities for materials were already set, and bidders entered their prices for various items.

The design-build concept is very different. In it, MnDOT and the contractor agree to a fixed price up front. The design and construction time overlap, shortening the completion time and often reducing cost. Construction begins before all design details are final, which accelerates response time and dispute resolution. Efficiencies accrue for quality, cost, and schedule from design through construction. Also, the project benefits from greater innovation and flexibility in selecting design, materials, and construction methods.

MnDOT was the first Minnesota public agency to receive design-build authority and had used the approach six times before the bridge collapsed. Some MnDOT PMs were more comfortable with the conventional low-bid, design-bid-build process and were hesitant to use this approach. However, with experience, results were increasingly positive. For instance, the $232 million project for Rochester's Highway 52 reported a calculated benefit/cost ratio of 1:58. This means that for every dollar invested, MnDOT estimated a $1.58 return in benefits from the reduced travel times, reduced number of crashes, savings in vehicle operating costs, and reduced roadway maintenance costs.

With the goal to restore the vital I-35W transportation link by the end of 2008, Chiglo's group decided to use a combination of best value and design-build approaches to stimulate speed of project delivery, design flexibility, and construction innovation.

A radical idea.

MnDOT and others involved in the project felt that the non-traditional approach would be beneficial. The hybrid approach would incentivize potential contractors to bring innovative solutions to rebuild the bridge and to do so in record time, on budget, and within quality and safety standards.

IN SEARCH OF EXCELLENCE

Chiglo's team set out to find the right partner—a contractor that accepted MnDOT's aggressive goals as its own and brought unique skills to the table. MnDOT sought a partner that understood the sensitive nature of the project—that is, that citizens were seeking a memorial place of honor as well as a transportation corridor. Further, the team wanted a partner that openly shared risk and reward for meeting clearly defined desired outcomes. Fortunately, the more progressive 2001 legislature allowed MnDOT to grant potential bidders substantial autonomy and flexibility to design a bridge that met the desired outcomes.

The first challenge required a request for proposal (RFP) that clearly spelled out MnDOT's desired outcomes. In order to meet the aggressive schedule, the team knew its specifications had to focus on the "what," not the "how."

The RFP deviated from tradition in that it allowed latitude for the contractors to apply their own ideas. MNDOT'S team stipulated high-level requirements, such as geometric layout, environmental requirements, drainage requirements, and a deadline for completion of December 24, 2008. The RFP allowed the bidders to choose from several bridge and wall types, propose geometric solutions to correct substandard elements, and develop visual quality components for the project.

In addition, the RFP clearly defined six specific desired outcomes potential bidders would need to meet:

1. Safety
    a. Provide a safe Project area for workers, the traveling public, community, environment, and emergency services during the execution of the Project.
    b. Provide a solution consistent with MnDOT design and construction standards.

    c. Provide a solution adaptable to the recovery efforts of the collapsed bridge.

2. Quality

    a. Implement a quality management system that ensures the requirements of the Project will be met or exceeded and ensure public confidence.

    b. Reduce future maintenance costs by providing a high-quality project.

3. Schedule

Complete construction by December 2008.

4. Environmental Compliance

Provide a quality product with minimal impacts to the environment while using context-sensitive solutions.

5. Budget

Implement innovative solutions to maximize the return on taxpayer investment by reducing costs and improving quality of the transportation system.

6. Aesthetics

Utilize visual quality techniques and context-sensitive design to incorporate the bridge into the surrounding environment.

Although the law granted suppliers a high degree of flexibility in how they designed and built the bridge, Chiglo and his team faced an interesting dilemma. The onus of public accountability precluded MnDOT from entering into a purist version of outcome-based approaches in key areas. One legitimate area MnDOT was required to dictate concerned safety precautions.

The second challenge Chiglo's team faced was putting together a fair bidding process. Just how would the team define *best value* and potentially justify a decision that might not award the business to the contractor with the lowest price? Low cost was important, but Chiglo and the team wanted to look beyond the bid price and factor in a critical element: the cost of time. Governor Pawlenty and the public made it clear that speed was an essential factor. They wanted the bridge to be open by Christmas Eve, less than 18 months after the collapse. For this reason, the evaluation criteria included number of days to complete the project as a specific factor in the formula. MnDOT assigned a "cost" of $200,000 for each day after December 24 that it took a contractor to complete the project. Fees for delay would be the responsibility of the contractor. The $200,000 was based on the estimated 50 percent of road user costs—a number the team felt was conservative relative to the overall cost impact of not having a bridge.

Chiglo's team developed an exhaustive plan to make certain the process was fair. It involved multiple committees and advisory groups and, ultimately, relied on a best value formula for selecting the winning bidder. The formula was comprised of a technical score, the number of days to complete the project, and the contract bid price.

$$(A) + (B \times \$200,000) \div \text{Technical Proposal Average Score}$$
$$= \text{Adjusted bid}$$

Where
A = contract bid price
B = number of days to complete project
$200,000 per day = economic impact of not having the bridge in place (The longer the bid took to complete, the higher the bid price.)
Technical Proposal Average Score = collective score of safety, quality, schedule, environmental compliance, budget, and aesthetics

The law mandated MnDOT follow an evaluation plan that assured fairness and uniformity. The process needed to protect taxpayer dollars as well as MnDOT itself. Chances were excellent Chiglo's team would be called on to legally justify why they did not select the lowest-price bidder.

To ensure transparency and objectivity in the selection process, MnDOT was required to list selection criteria for every stage of the process and the evaluation weight of each criterion. Chiglo and the technical review committee diligently followed this provision to ensure evenhandedness with the bidders.[4]

BORN TO BUILD

One of the proposals was from Flatiron Constructors, Inc., and Manson Construction Company, which formed a joint venture for the project. Flatiron is a leader in North America's construction and civil engineering industry. Its credentials include many segmental, bascule, cable-stayed, and suspension bridges with national landmark designations. Manson Construction is known for its professional workforce, many of whom are second-, third-, and fourth-generation workers who specialize in the construction of foundations, bridges, piers, and other marine facilities in the United States.

British-born Peter F. Sanderson was poised to lead the joint Flatiron–Manson team as project manager if the duo secured the bid. Sanderson, a professional engineer, has traveled the world for building projects since he was a boy. His father brought his family with him while working on power plants, railways, and bridges from the Netherlands to Australia to Iraq. Peter Sanderson continued the family profession, gaining global experience in heavy civil construction. On August 1, 2007, when the I-35W Bridge collapsed, Sanderson was managing a sea-link project in India. International television, however, gave him a front-row seat in the crumbling pavement and smoke-filled skies of Minneapolis. He knew immediately that he would be leaving India: "I knew about the state of infrastructure in the U.S. and wondered when something like this would happen. I believed, surely, there would be a lot of work to do. And I wanted to be part of bringing credibility back to bridge building."[5] Sure enough, not long after, Sanderson got the call to lead the team for Flatiron–Manson.

Flatiron–Manson also brought in two other important partners, Johnson Brothers and FIGG. Johnson Brothers is a heavy civil contractor with 80 years of experience specializing in bridge, highway, infrastructure, marine, industrial, and emergency construction services for both public and private clients. FIGG Engineering Group, led by president and world-renowned architect Linda Figg, is known for beautifully designed renowned landmark bridges across the country.

It was easy for the Flatiron–Manson team to understand what MnDOT wanted. The RFP was clear, spelling out exactly how much weight was given to each of MnDOT's desired outcomes. Specifications for the bridge itself were not so clear, a situation Flatiron–Manson and its architectural partner FIGG Engineering found refreshing. MnDOT was asking them to bring their brainpower, not just their lowest-priced bodies, to the project. The combination of clear definitions of the "what" and the absence of constraints on the "how" empowered the Flatiron–Manson team to develop a world-class proposal aimed at providing the best overall value for MnDOT.

Flatiron–Manson's solution was to construct a "concrete box girder variable depth superstructure with a sweeping parabolic curve stretching 504 feet over the Mississippi River," to quote from its website. This may not sound too impressive to nonengineers. But the fact that MnDOT allowed prospective contractors to have control over big design decisions was not the norm for public works projects.

In fact, it was a radical approach.

Flatiron–Manson welcomed the challenge. It felt strongly that it would provide the best overall value for MnDOT.

When the results were in, Flatiron–Manson's gut was correct. Its proposal was not the lowest price; in fact, it was the most expensive. Yet it met MnDOT's desired outcomes far better than any of the other proposals. In the end, MnDOT held true to its word, and less than 60 days after the tragedy, MnDOT and Flatiron–Manson sealed the deal with a formal contract.

Jon Chiglo explained why Flatiron–Manson was selected from the field of four primary contenders. "Flatiron–Manson, on paper, was the most expensive bid. But they brought skills to the table that were *needs, not wants.* Things like understanding of community buy-in and outreach to school kids. Some contractors allowed for a week to get this done; it took more like six months and was ongoing throughout the project. We could not ignore public perception and sensitivity to public relations. Flatiron–Manson understood this. At the end, 94 percent approved of the project and were happy with result. We needed the innovations, needed the smart bridge; we needed the beauty. This was a business investment that paid big dividends for the Minnesota citizens."

ACCOUNTABILITY TO INNOVATE

By contract, the I-35W St. Anthony Falls Bridge had to open to traffic by Christmas Eve 2008. For Flatiron–Manson to be successful, it needed to develop innovative and efficient solutions that met the aggressive deadline, stayed within budget, and met required safety and quality standards.

Flatiron–Manson was in control of its own destiny. In fact, the final contract language could not be more clear that it was Flatiron–Manson's responsibility to make and take ownership for major decisions. Section 5.1 of the contract read:

> Control and Coordination of Work: Contractor shall be solely responsible for and have control over the construction means, methods, techniques, sequences, procedures and Site safety, and shall be solely responsible for coordinating all portions of the

Work under the Contract documents, subject, however, to all
requirements contained in the Contract Documents.

This simple clause meant Flatiron–Manson was not entitled to
submit change orders—which was often the norm in construction projects and the cause of cost overruns. Flatiron–Manson
designed the bridge; it would have to build within the budget as
proposed.

Flatiron–Manson not only had accountability, but incentives
in the pricing model meant it shared both risks and rewards
based on performance. For example, if the bridge opened early,
Flatiron–Manson would get a bonus of $200,000 a day. If the
bridge opened late, the contractor would have to pay MnDOT
$200,000 a day. The more timely Flatiron–Manson was, the
more profit it could earn. Working around the clock and using
innovative approaches would be crucial to increase efficiencies
in how the company worked.

Flatiron–Manson was up to the challenge. Its team of experts
was excited about the freedom to innovate and infuse their own
expertise in their quest to meet MnDOT's desired outcomes.
These innovations included concrete, smart bridge technology,
and even design management techniques.

Setting Innovation in Concrete

Innovation was literally set in concrete. Flatiron–Manson and its
concrete partner, Cemstone Products Company, brought improved
casting processes, technology, and even mixing models.

In concrete casting, for example, Flatiron–Manson brought
innovative ideas. The new bridge was a totally concrete structure
with construction happening through the winter—a *Minnesota*
winter where temperatures often drop to below freezing. In general, concrete construction is delayed until spring, because concrete does not set well in the cold.

To describe Minnesota winters, writers use such phrases as "romantic," "stunningly beautiful," with "magical whiteness" and "pure as driven snow." Peter Sanderson remembers the first, full-out, no-restrictions day of work was Thanksgiving Day 2007, a frigid, windy, unfortunately typical Minnesota winter day. For the 400 to 600 local workers, a better adjective is "brutal." But Sanderson and his Flatiron–Manson crew persevered, building large hut-type structures into which they placed forms for the concrete. Heaters and fans were used to provide heat directly into the forms. Flatiron–Manson monitored and controlled temperatures so concrete could be poured and cured safely. It even installed heaters to prevent the ground from freezing.

Cold weather was not the only issue Flatiron–Manson faced when it came to the concrete. No matter how cold the outside temperature may be, a chemical reaction within fresh concrete creates heat that can compromise the integrity of the structure as the concrete cures. In the large back-span segments of the bridge—the sections of the bridge over land—controlling the curing process presented a real challenge. To avoid any problem, river water was pumped through narrow plastic PVC tubes inserted lengthwise into the poured concrete. The cold water dropped the temperature of the wet concrete and allowed optimum curing.

Eleven months of 24-hour construction meant work never stopped, no matter how low the temperature dropped or how strongly the winds blew. Flatiron–Manson used every strategy it could think of to protect the site and ensure forward momentum. Furnaces and hot air pumps abounded, of course. But other strategies were employed as well, such as building four temporary shelters that easily wheeled around the casting yard to protect newly poured concrete from the elements. Thermal blankets were used to protect both workers and construction elements. And, of course, individuals used face masks, hand warmers stuck inside mittens, and long underwear. Flatiron–Manson also brought in warming shelters for workers, but, hey, this was

Minnesota. Inclement weather, winter and summer, was just part of the deal.

On the surface, the decision to build a concrete bridge during winter might seem illogical. But a bridge constructed with structural concrete permitted the builders to be flexible. For starters, construction could begin before all the design work was completed. One such innovation Flatiron–Manson brought was in how the concrete forms were set. Usually, contractors buy one set of bridge pier forms and construct one pier at a time; Flatiron–Manson bought enough forms to construct all substructure elements simultaneously. To further shorten the time of construction, the back-span sections of the bridge were cast in place. On the construction site, less than half a mile south of the bridge, eight casting beds produced precast segments for the main spans, which were built over water. Typical practice uses only one or two casting beds. The location provided easy access for PMs and made it possible to work on all portions of the bridge deck at the same time. The precast segments eventually were moved into place using a large crane that transferred segments from the storage yard onto a flat-bottom barge, which then transported them upriver. The Manson Construction Company delivered the specialized expertise for this aspect of the project.

On May 25, 2008, nearly 1,000 spectators lined up to watch the first 200-ton segment be loaded on a barge to float downriver and be lifted into place. Talk about sidewalk supervisors!

Concrete innovation also came from the leadership of a subcontractor, Cemstone Products Company. Dr. Kevin A. MacDonald was charged with bringing innovative mixing techniques and ensuring that the concrete met quality standards despite being set during winter. MacDonald, Cemstone's vice president for engineering services, has a Ph.D. in engineering materials and welcomed the challenge.

There were several specific uses for concrete on the project, such as drilled shafts, footings, superstructure and deck, reinforcement and main span, and each had its own special mix. Specifications for concrete pavement vary widely depending on subgrade conditions, expected loading, anticipated pavement life span, available materials, and a myriad of other considerations. Under normal conditions, contractors develop concrete mixes with demanding specifications by creating trial mixes and testing them over time. However, there was no time for that on the I-35W project. Cemstone, based on previous experience, used mathematical modeling techniques to develop the mixes for the bridge. MacDonald's innovative mixing techniques passed the quality tests with flying colors. For example, when 5,000-pounds-per-square-inch compressive strength concrete was required, the concrete tested at 8,360 psi at 28 days and 9,890 psi at 56 days.

MacDonald also ensured the concrete used the most environmentally friendly techniques. He explained, "The new twist over the last 10 years has been to try to avoid materials that generate CO_2."[6] In his mixes, MacDonald used two industrial waste products—fly ash, left over from burning coal in power plants, and blast-furnace slag—to replace normal components of cement. The CO_2 emissions from these recycled products are accounted for within the initial electricity generation and steel manufacturing and thus help reduce the concrete's carbon footprint. An added benefit is concrete stronger than regular cement.

Flatiron–Manson's and Cemstone's creative approach to durability, fast-track building, and environmental responsibility on the I-35W St. Anthony Falls Bridge project went on to earn the 2010 Award of Excellence from the Portland Cement Association.

Smart Bridge Technology

Overall, MnDOT gave the architect/engineer freedom to design what *Popular Mechanics* magazine called "America's Smartest

Bridge." FIGG Engineering Group and Linda Figg, as primary architect, along with subcontractor Iteris, pushed the boundaries of intelligent design, that is, architecture in which computation and communication technologies are infused, seamlessly enhancing form with function. During construction, electronic sensors monitored the temperature of mass concrete placements. Sensors embedded in the drilled shafts and piers provided real-time information about stresses and movements resulting from the loads imposed by the cantilevered segments before they were joined together—research that will be helpful to future bridge projects around the globe.

But technology did not stop after construction was complete. A high-tech structural health monitoring system, equipped with 240 sensors that send data directly from the bridge to the University of Minnesota, was built into the structure to improve monitoring and reduce overall maintenance costs. The monitoring system covers five areas:

1. Support of construction processes
2. Record of structural behavior (structure monitoring) by MnDOT and the University of Minnesota
3. Control of the automated anti-icing system
4. Intelligent transportation system (traffic flow, traffic message signs, etc.)
5. Bridge security

Some argued that the sensors added costs, but they actually reduce overall bridge maintenance. For example, four different kinds of sensors evaluate the condition of surface wear and tear by measuring whether salt is penetrating the bridge deck pavement. Bridge repair and replacement are expensive, so early monitoring makes up for the initial cost of the sensors. Another type of meter measures pressure to keep track of the bridge's expansion joints and bearings. The University of Minnesota and MnDOT correlate that data with design codes to analyze how the bridge performs over its life span. Finally, wire strain gauges measure temperature as well as the amount of force per square inch placed on the concrete—all important in assessing a bridge's condition.

Another unique feature that would not have appeared if MnDOT had called all the shots is sculptures that eat air pollution. No kidding. The two sculptures are made of special photocatalytic concrete called TX Active. It reacts with ultraviolet light and pulls pollutant particles of carbon monoxide, sulfur dioxide, and nitrous oxide out of the air and converts them to less harmful substances. The sculptures contain a compound that makes them self-cleaning, so they should stay white for as long they stand.

As functional as the sculptures may be, they also add poignant beauty. Bathed in sunlight during day and ethereal blue light at night, they offer serendipitous greeting at both ends of the bridge. Three 30-foot wavy lines—a visual representation of the ancient, universal symbol for water—reach to the heavens, reflecting hope and sunlight.

Design Innovation

Many people think of innovation in terms of a product (such as concrete) or technology (such as the smart bridge technology). But innovation also came in the form of the design itself and community involvement.

One such example of design innovation came from Linda Figg. Flatiron–Manson teamed with FIGG Engineering Group to devise a masterful plan to get community involvement early. MnDOT and Flatiron–Manson knew it was important to get local community buy-in. The collapse had put MnDOT under intense scrutiny, and the public had a great deal of interest in the bridge rebuild. Community involvement was especially important since MnDOT was allowing Flatiron–Manson to control decisions regarding the actual type and design of the bridge.

After initial design gained approval from MnDOT, FIGG and Flatiron–Manson opened up the process to the public to help make the final design choices. FIGG used her copyrighted "Charette" process to provide an all-day community hearing on October 24, 2007. The process gave the public a chance to make choices between various design elements. Eighty-eight interested residents, business people, government officials, representatives of the cultural arts, the University of Minnesota community, and others gathered. Linda Figg led a highly interactive, highly visual process in which the community voted for its favorite design preferences, including a curved pier shape, open railing for new vistas, bridge color of white, native stone gabion walls, and feature lighting.

VESTED FOR SUCCESS

To say that the completed I-35W St. Anthony Falls Bridge is a winner is the ultimate understatement. MnDOT and the extended Flatiron–Manson team maneuvered the perilous path of multiple governments, overarching regulation, and conventional prescriptive procurement policies to create a stunning, quality-laden bridge. Together, they committed to each other's success to achieve mutually agreed-upon desired outcomes.

The agreement enhanced flexibility and innovation. The relationship drove efficient, effective decision making.

Colocation of the key partners paid big dividends. It enabled simplified communication, conflict resolution, and avoidance of misunderstandings. Chiglo insisted that "phone conversations and emails aren't sufficient. Communication works better when you're face to face. You can read body language, see the facial expressions, and just know the other person better.

Direct interaction minimizes misunderstandings and saves time."

Flatiron–Manson's Pete Sanderson and design counterpart Linda Figg agreed. Not only did they agree to open a joint office on site, the space also included MnDOT PMs and officials from the Federal Highway Administration and the Occupational Safety and Health Administration. Because the construction site was small, other key players had offices within walking distance. The objective was to ensure free flow of information, nonstop collaboration, and timely response to any situation that might arise.

Checks, rechecks, and widespread reporting were part of the daily regimen among Flatiron–Manson, FIGG, and MnDOT. These efforts facilitated catching and fixing any glitches early, baselines for continuous improvement, and necessary documentation.

"On a traditional job, when there are issues out in the field, typically the contractor comes to MnDOT and says, 'What do you want us to do?'" said Terry Ward, MnDOT's deputy manager for construction of the bridge. "On this job, when issues come up, we get together in a room and we talk about it—from the construction side, from the design, from our side—and we resolve it."[7]

Because the project was design-build, MnDOT's role was mainly to ensure that desired outcomes were met and to provide insight and advice for proactive problem solving. The nonstop collaboration helped the work flow more smoothly. It also built trust, an absolute necessity within any Vested relationship. Peter Sanderson explained simply, "It's the walk as opposed to the talk. Right from very beginning, when we had quality problems, we called MnDOT right away. 'This is the problem. This is what we're going to do about it.' We were proactive. We made sure we didn't hide anything. Mistakes were made. We rectified them.

We fixed it straight off the bat." The transparent approach built trust with the MnDOT team that facilitated progress.

The team constructed the $234 million I-35W St. Anthony Falls Bridge three months ahead of schedule and on budget, with no time lost due to safety accidents. The project has won over 20 awards for excellence, including the Federal Highway Administration's Award of Excellence, the FIATECH[8] Celebration of Engineering and Technology Innovation Award, and the National Council of Structural Engineers Association's Excellence in Structural Engineering Award.

MnDOT's success provides real insight into the power of focusing on the *what* and not the *how*.

4

U.S. DEPARTMENT OF ENERGY TRANSFORMS WEAPONS WASTELAND TO WILDLIFE SITE

If you don't know where you are going, you might not get there.

—*Yogi Berra*

RULE #3: CLEARLY DEFINED AND MEASURABLE DESIRED OUTCOMES

Baseball great Yogi Berra is often quoted for his folksy wit and funny but oddly apt takes on leadership and life. In one notable quote he said, "You've got to be very careful if you don't know where you're going, because you might not get there."

It is important to ask yourself (and answer) the question about where you are headed or, more concretely, what you hope to achieve by applying Vested principles.

Typically, desired outcomes include system-wide, high-level results for items such as lowered cost structures, higher service levels, higher market share, faster speed to market, reduced cycle time, more loyal customers, or more revenues.

The luxury carmaker Jaguar offers a good example of a desired outcome. Jaguar had been plagued with service parts issues for years. Remember the not-so-old joke that you used to have to own two Jaguars, one to drive and one waiting for parts? Jaguar set its eyes on moving from ninth to first in J. D. Power rankings for customer satisfaction. This meant beating archrivals Mercedes-Benz, BMW, and Lexus.

Vested relationships focus beyond an organization's own four walls, looking outward to others to help define and achieve success. For Jaguar, achieving the desired outcome meant partnering with a Unipart Logistics, a world-class supply chain management service provider. The two entered into a ten-year outsourcing agreement in 1998. Unipart invested heavily to transform Jaguar's supply chain with the goal to drive customer satisfaction. Year by year, Jaguar edged up in the J. D. Power rankings; it won the coveted award in 2007 and has continued to bring in high honors ever since.

Desired outcomes require business partners to work together to achieve success. Desired outcomes are *not* the task-oriented service-level agreements typically found in conventional supplier agreements. They are not simply about doing a task faster or getting a product cheaper. They are about the end game, getting results. They are about achieving transformation.

Of course, success in business is similar to success in life. Reflection and clear thinking are needed to find the right path. Vested Rule #3 seeks to direct your thinking and set you on a productive path. The highly lauded Department of Energy and Kaiser-Hill relationship to clean up the Rocky Flats nuclear weapon site depicts the kinds of things to think about when trying to define success and often hard-to-articulate desired outcomes.

ROCKY FLATS—COMING CLEAN IN COLORADO

The Atomic Energy Commission (AEC) authorized operations at the Rocky Flats plant in 1952 as a direct response to the U.S.–Russia Cold War escalation of nuclear weapons manufacture. It was part of what would come to be known as the policy of mutual assured destruction.[1] Workers at Rocky Flats processed, purified, and machined the plutonium pits that served as the triggers for nuclear weapons. Most of the workers were civilians who passed rigorous security clearances prior to assignment.

Working at Rocky Flats was a family tradition for Denny Ferrera, a metallurgist and supervisor. His dad started at the plant in 1952. Denny himself started in 1975, joining his twin brother, Kenny, and numerous cousins, as a research metallurgist for plutonium. Denny even met his wife at the plant. Altogether, over 20 members of the Ferrera family worked at Rocky Flats. The family—like all of the workers—took great pride in their jobs, believing their highly specialized skills manufacturing nuclear weapons was essential to counter the threat of the Soviet Union and the Cold War. In fact, Rocky Flats never missed a production quota and enjoyed the highest production quality of any Department of Energy (DOE) facility.[2]

At the height of production, the site operated 24/7 with nearly 8,000 employees producing what some claimed to be the deadliest devices ever invented.[3] It was the potential environmental hazards at Rocky Flats that caused concern among members of the Environmental Protection Agency (EPA). In fact, EPA had been in a fierce territorial battle with DOE over jurisdiction. DOE argued that the site was exempt from the Resource Conservation and Recovery Act because of "national security" and that it had sole authority to govern the facilities under the Atomic Energy Act. EPA—with authority to oversee the environment—believed that Rocky Flats did not meet federal safety standards, and the agency was determined to see DOE fully comply with regulations. Jeremy Karpatkin, the Rocky Flats director of communications and economic development from 1995 to 1999, described the magnitude of the tension between the groups. "If environmental regulators needed to inspect a tank inside a nuclear production building, armed guards would blindfold them and escort them inside. 'Distrust' doesn't quite characterize it. We're talking about overt, livid hostility."[4]

A flyover of Rocky Flats gave the Federal Bureau of Investigation (FBI), Justice Department, and EPA enough suspicion to launch a surprise raid—coined "Operation Desert Glow"—to investigate allegations of environmental crimes. Suspicions were confirmed, and the oversight agencies ordered Rocky Flats to shut down production in June 1989. President George H. W. Bush ultimately ordered full closure of Rocky Flats when he discontinued the W-88 warhead program in 1992.

Reports from the site were daunting. One report from the General Accounting Office (GAO; now the Government Accountability Office) to Congress explained the magnitude of the problem in layperson's terms: "The total amount of radioactive waste that the contractor is required to package and ship off-site is enough to fill a 19-story building the size of a football field." (A 2006 GAO postclosure report stated that the actual amount was the equivalent of a 65-story building the length and width of a football field.)[5]

The numbers were staggering. Twenty-one tons of weapons-usable nuclear materials needed to be removed, including plutonium, uranium, beryllium, tritium, carbon tetrachloride, and dioxin. Eight hundred buildings and structures needed to be decontaminated and/or demolished—over 3 million square feet of real estate. Thirty thousand liters of plutonium needed to be drained from tanks and pipes, some of which were known to be leaking. In total, 258,000 cubic meters of transuranic waste stored in 39,500 containers needed to be dealt with.[6] Making matters worse, Operation Desert Glow resulted in a "hot" shutdown of production. "It was like people just went to lunch midshift and never came back. The improper shutdown left hazardous materials in pipelines and hot workstations, making cleanup very tenuous," explained Ferrera.[7]

DOE faced what many called an impossible task. Total closure and cleanup of a nuclear production facility had never been accomplished anywhere in the world. No one was certain how it could be done. The official DOE 1995 Baseline Environmental Management Report estimated that the project could require up to 75 years and cost up to $37 billion.[8] Other estimates ranged from $17 billion to $100 billion and from 65 years to 100 years.[9] While some might argue the early projections were simply a shot in the dark, one thing is clear: The cleanup and closure of Rocky Flats was a formidable task.

By 1995, Congress and DOE were frustrated. Two different contractors had made little progress toward cleanup since the 1989 raid. DOE determined it was time to try a different approach. Could it find a way to clean up and close Rocky Flats in half the time? Or even one-fourth of the time? Just how clean could the site be made? And did the job really have to cost $37 billion?

On July 1, 1995, DOE signed a five-year contract with Kaiser-Hill Company LLC, a joint venture between CH2M Hill and Kaiser Engineers, to manage Rocky Flats. The agreement named Kaiser-Hill the integrating management contractor of four primary subcontractors, including Rocky Mountain Remediation Services (waste operations, decontamination and decommissioning, environmental restoration); Safe Sites of Colorado (plutonium stabilization, repackaging, consolidation, accountability of special nuclear materials, highly enriched uranium shipments, classified parts management agreement); Wackenhut Services, Inc. (security); and DynCorp of Colorado, Inc. (building management, maintenance, medical, and emergency preparedness). The first order of business was to get the 3,644 contractor personnel working, protect the site safely, and design a comprehensive closure plan.

The contract, the first performance-based contract for DOE, had significant incentives tied to worker safety, unquestioned quality, budget compliance, and reducing the time needed to complete the project.[10]

Nancy Tuor, a CH2M Hill executive, was a key leader for Kaiser-Hill from beginning to end. From taking on the responsibility to transform the culture—both internal and external—to accepting the $257 million final incentive check as chief executive, Tuor remembered it all clearly. "The old management and operation contracts were egregious in their waste and inefficiency. It offended my sensibilities as a taxpayer. How can you have a project that lasts longer than your children? Kaiser-Hill was excited at the opportunity to work under a performance-based contract. We welcomed the challenge to bring innovations that could radically reduce the costs and time needed to close the site."[11]

Tuor helped put together a team of 41 people (20 on-site workers, 10 Kaiser-Hill managers, 10 CH2M Hill managers, and 1 DOE executive) who went off site for eight weeks to answer this basic question: What can we do for $5 billion and in five years if we have no rules?

The report came back suggesting total cleanup and closure in seven years and at a cost of $7 billion. Tuor reported, "They blew our mind away. We told them no rules and they really followed that. It was stunning to see the ideas they came up with and how they really turned the strategy upside down. From that day on, the debate changed. The mind-set changed from 'do what we are told' to 'don't tell me it can't be done.' We literally created the beginnings of a culture where the answer is never *no* but rather *what will have to happen to make it possible?*"

In 2005, just ten short years after Kaiser-Hill took over the project, the improbable became a reality: Rocky Flats and adjoining formerly contaminated land were transformed into a 6,550-acre wildlife refuge. The site was not just clean but clean enough for birds and bison. The project also came in a staggering $27 billion under the initial budget projections and 65 years ahead of initial projections.[12]

This rest of this chapter tells the remarkable story of how DOE and Kaiser-Hill worked together to achieve success and save taxpayers billions.

IT STARTS WITH A VISION

By the time Kaiser-Hill took over the management of Rocky Flats, Congress was concerned and angry. President Bush made it clear in 1992 that Rocky Flats was no longer in the business of making weapons. Although the site was standing idle, it was still draining almost a billion taxpayer dollars a year just to keep it safe while DOE tried to come up with a plan for its cleanup and closing. Tuor remembers looking at the budget and being amazed. "Out of the $850 million budget, $800 million was for just maintaining it safely. The security bill alone was $100 million a year."

For DOE and Kaiser-Hill to be successful, they needed a vision for closing down Rocky Flats. The book *Making the Impossible Possible* reports a statement from a congressional staff member describing the importance of establishing a vision from the onset.

> Everyone had been aligned about how horrible this waste was here. We were never going to get rid of it. It was going to contaminate our water systems and imperil a city the size of Denver for the next hundred years....Leadership had to convince people they were part of something really big—something that would be the highlight of their career and highlight of their life.[13]

But finding that clear vision was a challenge. Multiple government organizations had varying degrees of jurisdiction over Rocky Flats. A myriad of initialed government agencies, including the AEC, CDPHE, EPA, and NAEC, weighed in with opinions.[14]

Faced with formidable challenges, the parties set out to create an aligned vision that would become a beacon of what the future looked like. To assure buy-in, the public was invited to a series of meetings to discuss the cleanup and generate ideas for the future use of the site. Along the way, the idea to create a wildlife refuge emerged. The parties would be successful if they could turn one of the most toxic sites in the world into a wildlife refuge. From weapons to wildlife.

It was a radical idea.

What emerged was an overarching vision, something bigger than any individual or group. It was transformational. People were part of doing what had never been done before—successful decontamination, demolition, and disposal of dangerous buildings and hazardous waste and eventual transformation of the land back to prairie as a wildlife refuge. The stakes were huge, and so was the pride for those who were making it happen.

A contest to rename the project was created to honor the vision and vest community input, and the Rocky Flats Environmental Technology Site was born. Finally, on July 19, 1996, the State of Colorado, EPA, and DOE signed the Rocky Flats Cleanup Agreement, formalizing the vision statement that pointed to the path to success:

> Be the model site for environmental cleanup and economic conversion with community recognition and support.

The vision was good, but Kaiser-Hill leaders felt strongly that they needed to simplify the vision to a rallying cry for the entire workforce. The result? The simple mantra of "Not a day late, not a dollar more." This slogan aligned with DOE and Kaiser-Hill's time and money objectives and incentivized employees, who learned that Kaiser-Hill would share up to 20 percent of its earnings with workers who helped meet the goals.

The agreement established the regulatory framework for achieving the cleanup of the site and established three clearly defined desired outcomes.

1. Ensure that Rocky Flats does not pose an unacceptable risk to the citizens of Colorado or to the site's workers from either contamination or an accident.
2. Achieve accelerated cleanup and closure of Rocky Flats in a safe, environmentally protective manner and in compliance with applicable state and federal environmental laws.
3. Work toward disposition of contamination, wastes, buildings, facilities, and infrastructure from Rocky Flats consistent with community preference and national goals.

Simply put, the agreement meant that Rocky Flats needed to be safely cleaned and closed.

DOE leaders, such as project managers Mark Silverman and Jesse Roberson, recognized that government bureaucracy and normal procedures were likely obstacles to success and fought for the agreement to include language that would break long-established practices. For example, the agreement specified that the parties would:

Seek ways to accelerate cleanup actions and *eliminate unnecessary tasks* and reviews, by requiring that the Parties to the Agreement work *together.*

Provide the *flexibility* to modify the work scope and schedules, recognizing that priorities of specific tasks and schedules *may change* as the cleanup progresses due to emerging information on Site conditions, risk priorities, and available resources. [Emphasis added.][15]

The first parameter kept both parties engaged with the cleanup process and stressed the importance of working together. The second, which manded flexibility, acknowledged that DOE knew it did not know everything about the site and what it would take to clean it. This wise provision proved helpful on several occasions. One example is when DOE decided to change the definition of "clean" for areas of soil outside the contaminated building area from 651 picocuries per gram of radiation (pCi/gm)[16] to just 50 pCi/gm based on community input.

Creating a flexible framework with high incentives was not standard operating procedure for government work. In fact, many critics feared Kaiser-Hill would cut corners to earn the incentives. To mitigate this risk, DOE defined measurable desired outcomes, making it clear that cutting cost did not mean weakening standards. DOE then carefully aligned incentives to the desired outcomes, ensuring Kaiser-Hill's *desire* to not just work fast but to innovate to cut fat and waste out of processes *while still meeting safety and cleanup standards.*

CLEARLY DEFINED AND MEASURABLE DESIRED OUTCOMES

A Vested relationship always contains performance metrics that clearly define and measure success against desired outcomes. These outcomes are the result of collaboration to establish crystal-clear understanding of how to define success. Careful construction of desired outcomes and associated metrics creates the road map the relationship follows to stay on track for success. For Rocky Flats, success was defined as safely cleaning up and closing the site as cost effectively as possible. Each of the desired outcomes—safe, clean, closed, and costs—will now be explored in more detail.

Desired Outcome: Safety First

Under the agreement, Kaiser-Hill was required to use the existing workforce—a workforce that had been embedded in Rocky Flats since 1952. For the workers, Rocky Flats was far more than a waste site. It was their life's work. The workers were proud of their role in winning the Cold War and were confused and frustrated by what they believed was an overly anxious outside world. Denny Ferrera reflected on the workers' mood after the FBI raid. "After the shutdown, DOE informed us that all the policies and procedures needed to change. Overnight we were told everything we knew and had done in the past was wrong. It was very demoralizing and depressing. After the raid, the workers spent all of their time writing and rewriting procedures and working out 'conflicts of procedure.'" When Nancy Tuor walked on the job her first day, she learned the workforce was more than just demoralized; they were also angry and had over 900 grievances on file.[17]

One of the reasons was safety. Rocky Flats had a poor safety record, including holding the dubious record of, in 1969, having the worst industrial fire in the history of the United States. In 1994, Building 771 had been called the "most dangerous building in America" during an *ABC Nightline News* broadcast.[18] Rocky Flats scored well below DOE and construction industry averages for safety metrics when Kaiser-Hill took over in 1995. The 12-month rolling average for total recordable cases (the number of occupation-related incidents requiring more than basic first aid) in July 1995 was 7.6, above the construction industry average of 6.4 and the contractually obligated 3.5. Another key measure of safety— lost workdays (restricted days away from work)—was at 4.6 in July 1995, well above the construction industry average of 2.4 and the contract target of 2.0.[19]

Because the original Rocky Flats employees would accomplish the cleanup, both DOE and Kaiser-Hill knew worker morale and safety issues needed to change if the parties were to be successful. DOE did not expect changes overnight, but it did expect changes. Tuor explained the importance of a new way of thinking: "We needed to change the culture and that needed to start with a strong safety culture, a cooperative approach between management and workers, a collaborative approach with regulators, and innovative approaches in employee motivation."[20]

The organizations agreed to use an approach known as an organization diagnosis survey to establish a performance baseline on four factors. The tool measured Kaiser-Hill senior managers' influence on the productivity of Rocky Flats workers. If Kaiser-Hill was making a difference, the workers would know it. The four performance factors became a key part of the contract, with Kaiser-Hill required to close the gap between current performance and the desired outcome. The goal was for Kaiser-Hill to be in the top 30 percent across each of the four performance factors compared to other projects/contractors under the DOE umbrella.

Tuor is proud of the results shown in the performance comparison. By the end of the project, Kaiser-Hill had reduced a backlog of 900 employee grievances to a mere handful. In safety measures, Kaiser-Hill completed 60+ million hours of work with no life-threatening injuries or environmental releases. It improved the total recordable case safety rate from 7.6 to 0.9 per full-time equivalent employee. And the lost workday rate dropped from 4.6 to 0.2, a full 75 percent below other DOE sites and well below the construction industry average of 2.4.[21] In fact, the rate was so low that Kaiser-Hill earned a $300,000 rebate from its insurance company for the superior safety record.[22] The following chart depicts the four performance factors.

Figure 4.1   Performance Comparison

Performance Factor	Rocky Flats 1995	30% Threshold Score to Be at the Top of the Industry	Baseline Difference
(1)	(2)	(3)	Base of Comparison (3)–(2)
Accountability	4.27	5.14	0.87
Productivity	3.91	4.88	0.97
Quality	3.61	4.93	1.32
Safety	5.0	6.10	1.10

Desired Outcome: Closed

Although safety was paramount, getting Rocky Flats closed was job #1. However, Kaiser-Hill's 1995 contract did not specify a closure date for good reason. How could DOE hold Kaiser-Hill accountable for closure when the contract was for only five years, much less than the time needed to complete the actual closure? In addition, noncompetitive contract extensions were not standard practice. There was no guarantee that Kaiser-Hill would be awarded future work on the Rocky Flats project when the project came up for bid again.

Most commercial and contract managers would fear the level of ambiguity in the DOE/Kaiser-Hill contract. But DOE and Kaiser-Hill viewed it as an asset. Tuor explained the rationale: "Milestones could be set enabling the parties to get a better understanding of the work to be done, and at what costs. This approach minimized the impact of unknown factors affecting the cost. And it was a more fair approach than merely shifting risks to Kaiser-Hill."

Even though DOE did not include a closure date in the first contract, it did realize that time was money. For that reason, DOE linked a significant portion of Kaiser-Hill's compensation to incentives for completing deliverables needed to progress toward closure activities. For example, in the contract's first fiscal year, Kaiser-Hill's base fee was $2,734,665. To motivate speed and accomplishment, the available performance-based incentive fee was $15,496,435, about 5.5 times the base.

DOE's decision to adopt its first ever performance-based contract paid off. Properly structuring incentives around clearly defined desired outcomes and metrics worked. Kaiser-Hill, enlisting the help of the skilled workforce already in place, created innovative approaches to increase safety levels and efficiency and met or beat almost every metric in the first contract.

Due to excellent performance, DOE signed a new contract with Kaiser-Hill that took effect February 1, 2000, for $3.94 billion.[23] That's right! The contract meant revenue in the *billions*, compared to the first of several million dollars. This time there was a firm deadline for completion: December 15, 2006. Kaiser-Hill was accountable for demolishing more than 700 structures that remained and cleaning up the site's contaminated soil and groundwater. The contract was the first ever DOE performance-based contract that *shared risks as well as incentives*.

It is interesting to note DOE increased its use of incentives in the 2000 contract with Kaiser-Hill, including groundbreaking provisions for incentives *and* penalties. A 70/30 percent split was negotiated for cost savings. For every dollar Kaiser-Hill saved under the $3.94 billion target costs of the contract, it could keep 30 percent and the American taxpayers would keep 70 percent. Additional incentives were tied to early completion. Conversely, if Kaiser-Hill failed to meet deadlines or cost targets, penalties applied. It was risky business for Kaiser-Hill, but it was up to the challenge.

Why offer additional incentives? DOE reaped significant benefits from an early closing. The sooner the extraordinary health and safety risks were mitigated, the better. Plus, completing the project early meant decreased operating costs during those out years. For instance, the savings from not requiring security at the site was over $100 million per year.[24] Simply put, paying incentives put extra dollars into the pockets of Kaiser-Hill and the Rocky Flats employees. But with a 70/30 split, DOE was poised to return even more dollars to taxpayers—billions more. According to Assistant Energy Secretary James Rispoli, the financial incentives for speed and performance built into the DOE contract with Kaiser-Hill were of particular importance. Rispoli told a Senate Energy and Commerce Committee hearing, "This contract was clearly the flagship in being innovative in this approach."[25]

A true win-win-win.

Everyone celebrated when Kaiser-Hill finished the job ahead of schedule on October 13, 2005, and received an additional $170 million incentive fee, which raised its total incentives to an impressive $560 million.[26]

Desired Outcome: Cleaned Up

A close date might be easy to measure, but there was more debate about how to measure "clean." Without a reference point, how do you know what "clean" means? Consider any teenager told to clean her room, and the definitions could fill a book. How clean would Rocky Flats have to be? Just how would success be defined?

The rationale for setting standards for each identified source of contamination was to provide a signal for what success meant. One of the most emotional and contentious arguments regarded the definition of acceptable levels of soil contamination. The 1996 Cleanup Agreement among DOE, EPA, and the Colorado Department of Public Health initially defined the "clean" target of 651 pCi/gm for soil samples outside the building area, a target that left Rocky Flats substantially more contaminated than many Pacific Island atomic bomb test sites after government-mandated cleanup.

Two stakeholder community groups—the Rocky Flats Citizens Advisory Board and the Rocky Flats Coalition of Local Governments—did not feel the levels were acceptable and argued for much more stringent measures. One board member voiced the public passion: "You know, this whole issue about what the cleanup level's gonna be. I don't get that. I'm like, are you gonna clean it up or are you not gonna clean it up. If I can go out there with a Geiger Counter when you're gone, am I gonna get a click?"[27]

DOE and Kaiser-Hill responded, with DOE funding a community-directed, independent scientific assessment of soil action levels overseen by a panel of community representatives. The parties ultimately agreed to a revised measure of 50 pCi/gm. (For reference, a plutonium level of 50 pCi/gm translates to a risk level of 1 in 500,000 for a wildlife worker working on the site. In other words, this level of contamination could result in one more case of cancer than otherwise would have been expected in every 500,000 persons.) The 2000 contract upped the ante for Kaiser-Hill and lowered the pCi targets. Throughout the project, hundreds of confirmation samples were taken. Kaiser-Hill once again delivered with results far below even the more stringent requirements. Upon completion, the mean value of the remaining plutonium contamination in the remediated sections was 14 pCi/gm.[28]

The changing soil contamination target is just one example of how fluid the agreement needed to be. With a wry smile, Tuor explained, "The goalposts moved every day—because we kept finding surprises. We called it the discovery channel. Requirements continuously changed as lessons were learned. We came to realize once a problem could be identified, we had the creative resources to solve it. A unique aspect of the contract was that the incentives aligned the interests of Kaiser-Hill with the interests of DOE. Kaiser-Hill was incentivized to meet the challenges. So when there were surprises or changes, we embraced them rather than fought them."

Desired Outcome: Cost

It's worth repeating: the cost estimates to complete the project were staggering—ranging from $17 billion to $100 billion. Traditional government contracts were cost plus, which meant DOE would pay for the costs and pay a prenegotiated fee or margin to the service provider. The hazardous environment increased costs as contractors frequently cited "safety" as the reason for "slow." DOE knew this common approach did not align contractors' interests with its interest to reduce costs. In fact, it created a perverse incentive because the higher the cost, the more money the contractor stood to make. Before 1989, fewer than 3,500 people were employed at Rocky Flats. Between 1989 (after production ceased) and 1995, employment jumped to 8,000. DOE purposefully aligned Kaiser-Hill's interest to reduce the overall costs by creating incentives directly tied to how well the company reduced them. The more money Kaiser-Hill saved DOE and taxpayers, the more profit Kaiser-Hill could earn.

A GAO report lauded Kaiser-Hill for developing over 200 innovations that saved the taxpayers billions of dollars. The report shared numerous example of how workers developed innovative cleanup technologies that accomplished tasks more safely, quickly, and cheaply.[29] Denny Ferrera agreed, saying, "Kaiser-Hill reengaged the workforce. They respected us and kept us informed through 'All Hands Meetings.' Gradually, the pride of being craftsmen came back, and we were eager to find answers to problems that emerged. Entire groups would come together to toss around ideas. One worker even developed a new packaging prototype in his garage at home on weekends which saved us hundreds of millions of dollars."

One example of this ingenuity solved the problem of airborne contamination. Rocky Flats had dozens of rooms with extreme levels of such contamination. Workers came up with the idea of spraying the rooms with an aerosol fog consisting of sugar, glycerin, and water with a fluorescent tracer. The fog attracted the radioactive materials, which sank to the floor. The fluorescent tracer made it easier to detect the location of the materials for cleanup. Ferrera explained how ingenious the idea was: "Removing toxins from surfaces is much easier than removing it from the air. Using this approach saved us billions of dollars. It is so effective the technology has been adopted around the world at other DOE sites."

Other innovations included new methods for dismantling glove boxes—not the small compartments on the passenger's side of a car, but stainless steel boxes up to 64 feet in length and with a capacity of more than 20,000 gallons. When the site was operational, workers forged trigger parts for nuclear weapons in the glove boxes, which included lead-lined gloves, acrylic viewing windows, and specialized shielding. The 1,475 glove boxes, which trapped neutron radiation inside and away from the workers, were some of the most contaminated items at Rocky Flats.

More than 1,475 glove boxes required decontamination at Rocky Flats, a dangerous and tedious process. To safely rid the site of contaminated glove boxes, the common practice was for workers to construct protective tents and use plasma torches to cut the boxes into pieces small enough to fit into special protective crates for transport to DOE's official Waste Isolation Pilot Plant 26 miles east of Carlsbad, New Mexico, which is licensed to permanently dispose of transuranic radioactive waste for 10,000 years.

Employees found a way to reduce the glove box contamination level to less than 100 nanocuries per gram, which enabled the boxes to be reclassified as low-level waste. Kaiser-Hill invented a process that uses a series of chemical sprays to neutralize and/or transform the toxic chemicals. For example, a cerium nitrate solution was developed that allowed radioactive pollutants inside the boxes to be wiped off contaminated containers and glove boxes. Harmful contamination was transferred to the wipe-off rags, which were easily packaged and shipped for disposal as transuranic waste. No matter what size, the glove boxes were left intact, and packaged for shipment to preauthorized low-level nuclear waste storage sites. This eliminated the need to cut up the boxes' stainless walls into small pieces and prevent escaping substances from entering the general workplace. The new process not only was much safer for the workers; it also increased the speed of glove box decontamination by a factor of 25.[30]

Sometimes, efficiencies resulted from simple common sense and thinking differently. Ferrera recalled Building 886, a lab with thick concrete walls. "Tearing the building down was a painstakingly slow process, chipping out walls—small areas at a time. One of the engineers suggested we find a way to use explosive demolitions to fracture and weaken the walls. This enabled us to use to pull the building down mechanically with big equipment. It was safe and saved us months of work. I was proud to be part of a workforce that could meet any challenge put before us."

The benefits of aligning Kaiser-Hill's goals and incentives to the government's desired outcome of cost reduction speak for themselves in terms of dollar savings. The official GAO post-cleanup report calculated the total cost of the cleanup was about $10 billion between 1995 and 2005—a whopping $27 billion under the baseline estimate.[31]

Measuring Success

Safety, cleanup, closure, and cost were the primary desired outcomes, but DOE did have other objectives and metrics. The original contract signed in 1995 outlined nine primary objectives of the project and included 60 metrics. A general description, performance measure, and incentive were specified for each objective. By 1999, the number of metrics had been reduced to 19 as DOE learned that focusing on the "critical few" generated better results.

Effective and consistent reporting was also key to the project. Kaiser-Hill's profit hinged on how well it performed, and all parties needed to have an objective way to measure success. One such example was how DOE measured successful closure activities. Kaiser-Hill developed an integrated system of project databases and monthly reports. DOE and Kaiser-Hill agreed to use a technique known as earned value (EV) to trigger payments to the company. Standard industry techniques for calculating EV provided a quantitative dollar value of work scope completed to facilitate assessment of project progress. Actual start dates, finish dates, and remaining duration for initiated cost accounting activities were posted to the project schedule. Actual costs were calculated by using budgeted cost of work scheduled (BCWS), budgeted cost of work performed (BCWP or EV), and actual cost of work performed (ACWP). The formula, BCWP – ACWP, calculated cost and schedule variances. Here is how it worked:

- The Kaiser-Hill executive management team selected a set of mission activities as part of the Rocky Flats baseline submittal.
- EV was earned only when the mission activity was 100 percent complete.

- Schedule variance compared the dollar amount of the mission activities planned to be 100 percent complete to the actual value of mission activities that were 100 percent complete each quarter.

To validate performance, DOE commissioned the U.S. Army Corps of Engineers, PricewaterhouseCoopers, and Ernst & Young to perform external credibility reviews. These neutral third-party reviews strengthened major stakeholders' confidence and increased the trust between Kaiser-Hill and DOE. The parties learned to work together as they explored how to achieve the impossible. The neutral third-party reviews mitigated the ability of either party to finger-point and set an overall tone of fairness. The external performance reviews also served to document Kaiser-Hill's exceptional performance and justified the incentive payments.

Flexible Framework

One of the advantages of the contract was its built-in flexibility. With all of the uncertainty about how, and if, success could be achieved, the contract had to be flexible and fair, with details figured out as the project proceeded. Flexibility and fairness were important for two reasons. First, it gave Kaiser-Hill the ability to make decisions and find innovations about how the work was done to best meet the objectives. For example, when dealing with nuclear production and hazardous waste, by law much of the work had to be done within specific safety requirements and federally mandated risk rankings. Although DOE established the risk rankings, the contract gave Kaiser-Hill flexibility in *how* it met the requirements as long as it adhered to the law.

An excellent example of this comes from a series of calculated actions Kaiser-Hill took to send a message that Rocky

Flats would no longer be run by a class system; the traditional plethora of perks for management was discontinued. Nancy Tuor shared the rationale. "We believed in symbolism and determined steps to prove things were going to be different. For example, we removed all the special parking places. No one had reserved parking any longer. Next, Kaiser-Hill made a strategic choice to remove the administration building first, which was a lower-priority site for DOE. By demolishing the administration building before any others, it made the point that we were all in this together. We moved senior management to a shared workspace in the middle of the action. Demolishing the building fostered trust as it demolished the historical separation between 'us' and 'them' and established new lines of communication between the workers and the new Kaiser-Hill management team. It is hard to talk about 'them' when they are in the same room."[32]

Denny Ferrera concurred. "We knew something was significantly different when we came to work during the first days and found the old guard shacks completely removed. As time went on, Kaiser-Hill made progress on two fronts— contamination cleanup of the interior of buildings and demolishment of building structures themselves. Most people couldn't see the progress inside buildings, so the changing skyline really helped everyone know progress was being made. For me, it was when the water tower went down. I could see the tower from the back deck of my house, so it really hit home."[33]

The second advantage of the flexibility was that it allowed DOE and Kaiser-Hill to set appropriate targets and incentives as they learned more. DOE could not realistically set some targets, such as the closure date, at the beginning of the project. In other cases, the targets were changed—such as in the level of allowable pCi targets for soil. DOE decided to set targets annually as the project revealed itself and its confidence in the value of incentives to reward Kaiser-Hill grew.

YOU GET WHAT YOU PAY FOR

With the Rocky Flats site cleanup, DOE learned an important lesson that many people might think of as common sense: You get what you pay for. Clearly defined and measurable desired outcomes with significant incentives motivated Kaiser-Hill not just to show up but to be wildly successful. DOE and Kaiser-Hill carefully crafted a relationship in which both parties were Vested. The more Kaiser-Hill achieved DOE's goals, the more Kaiser-Hill itself succeeded.

Of course, getting what you pay for is not something that happens automatically between a company and a supplier. In the case of Rocky Flats, Kaiser-Hill made a conscious decision to align worker goals and objectives to DOE/Kaiser-Hill's objectives. And Kaiser-Hill it put its money where its mouth was, committing to share 20 percent of any earned incentive fees with Rocky Flats employees. The individual incentives motivated employees to work safer, faster, and smarter. In addition, the incentive program provided a $5 million program to train and transition 4,000+ to new jobs. Ferrera explained the irony: "On one hand, we were working ourselves out of jobs with the closure of Rocky Flats. But on the other hand, we were creating history and earning incentives that would enable us to start a new chapter in our lives."

The Ferrera family is testament to how effective these efforts were. Denny is now the chief operating officer of CH2M Hill's nuclear business group, and his twin, Kenny, is a project manager in the same division. Denny's nephew, once a Rocky Flats fireman, took advantage of training opportunities and started up his own water backflow prevention business. Denny's wife, who once worked in the finance department, took her incentive checks and decided to be a stay-at-home mom.

VESTED FOR SUCCESS

Under their Vested relationship, DOE and Kaiser-Hill collaborated in a ten-year effort to transform the Rocky Flats site from weapons to wildlife. The official GAO postcleanup report calculated the total cost of the cleanup was about $10 billion—slashing $27 billion and 65 years from initial estimates.[34] The site was effectively decontaminated. The Citizens Advisory Board claimed victory when "infinity rooms" (rooms so badly contaminated, pollutant levels could not be measured) were safely decontaminated and demolished and soil contamination levels came in at 14 pCi/gm, 72 percent below the revised target of 50pCi/gm.

Nancy Tuor was pleased. Employee morale had shifted from disgruntled to delighted. The backlog of 900 employee grievances was reduced to a mere handful by end of contract. The total recordable case safety rate declined from 7.6 to 0.9. But probably the most impressive accomplishment were the over 200 innovations the workers generated, resulting in billions of dollars in savings for DOE that benefited not only the Rocky Flats project but other DOE sites as well.

Senator Wayne Allard summed up the success of Rocky Flats nicely: "Kaiser-Hill [made] the impossible, possible."[35] The site was and continues to be the largest, most complex environmental cleanup project in world history. Even Patrick Malone—the activist who spent nine months living in a tepee that blocked the railroad tracks to Rocky Flats—approved. He donated the tepee to the Rocky Flats Cold War Memorial. It now stands tall as a testament to all that made the wildlife refuge possible, from early protesters to final cleanup workforce.[36]

The project has won dozens of awards, including the 2006 the Project Management Institute's Project of the Year award. According to the institute, the project:

- Removed more than 21 tons of weapons-usable nuclear materials
- Decontaminated and demolished 800 structures, comprising more than 3 million square feet
- Drained 30,000 liters of plutonium solutions
- Dismantled and removed more than 1,450 contaminated production glove boxes and 700 tanks
- Stabilized and packaged 100 tons of high-content plutonium residue
- Performed environmental cleanup actions at 130 sites
- Dispositioned millions of classified items and excess property
- Safely shipped more than 600,000 cubic meters of radioactive waste to DOE-approved radioactive waste storage sites—enough to fill a string of railcars 90 miles long

Other accolades include three awards from the Construction Management Association of America and DOE's 2006 Project of the Year. *National Geographic* called Rocky Flats "DOE's poster child for cleanup success."[37]

For the Ferrera family, what is more satisfying than the awards and accolades is seeing eagles nesting in protected areas and wildlife scampering through mature prairie grass. The same place that once inspired anger and angst now is a peaceful countryside. Ferrera reflected on the impact of what he and his fellow workers at Rocky Flats accomplished. "It's strange to recall that a decade ago visitors were required to go through personal background investigations and as many as four checkpoints, complete with burly guards carrying loaded machine guns, to stand on the same ground." He chuckled as he related a story of a family trip to his brother's house. "We were driving by the Rocky Flats site, and I pointed out the window and told my eight-year-old daughter, 'That is where Mommy and Daddy used to work.' She answered, 'You used to be farmers?'"

It is important to understand that DOE's and Kaiser-Hill's efforts were not easily accomplished. There were stops and starts, depressing backslides, and magnificent breakthroughs. Radically beating cost, time, cleanliness, and safety projections involved fearlessness, commitment, and a leap of faith. It took fresh thinking and a Vested mind-set whereby the objectives of DOE and Kaiser-Hill became tightly aligned in each other's mutual success. Across the board, the Rocky Flats cleanup effort applied the Five Rules of Vested thinking, starting with a What's-In-It-For-We approach that is evident within every stakeholder group from the very top all the way down to the lowest-level employee and back up again.

Nancy Tuor is now CH2M Hill's group president and corporate sponsor for sustainability. She summed up the extensive collaboration efforts in this way: "The safe accelerated closure of Rocky Flats is a tribute to the tireless efforts of our dedicated and immensely talented workforce. This is the same workforce that helped win the Cold War and then demonstrated great flexibility and skill by transitioning to a world-class nuclear decommissioning workforce. These workers, in partnership with community leaders, elected officials, regulators, and many other committed individuals, have delivered this historic accomplishment for the people of Colorado and the U.S. Government."[38]

The government issued an 18-page, photo-filled brochure called "Rocky Flats—A Proud Legacy, A New Beginning." Books and articles were written about the achievement. The

Rocky Flats experience was expressed best in this simple sentence found within the DOE legacy closure project report:

> It is the sincere hope of everyone involved with the Rocky Flats Closure Project that the legacy of Rocky Flats will not be "Look what we did here" but rather, "Look what started here."[39]

MICROSOFT AND ACCENTURE PERFECT A PRICING MODEL

Most procurement professionals are hard-wired to win. The problem is that Microsoft's conventional definition of winning means that if Microsoft wins, the supplier loses. For Microsoft to succeed, we needed to redefine winning.

—Tim McBride, Microsoft's general manager of finance operations and former chief procurement officer

RULE #4: PRICING MODEL WITH INCENTIVES

Probably no other topic creates as much apprehension between two companies as trying to determine a fair price. The conventional procurement process pits buyers and sellers on opposite sides of the table. Classic negotiations training uses trade-offs and concessions as tactics to get the best possible price (or preserve as much margin as possible if you are a supplier). A win for the supplier means a loss for the buyer. The result? A zero-sum game and a mind-set in which the parties fight over taking bigger slices of the pie instead of combining their talents to make a bigger pie.

In many respects, getting to a win-win pricing relationship is the heart of Vested agreements because it speaks directly to the bottom line of the enterprise and its ultimate success. But how exactly do you establish a pricing model to foster a win-win relationship?

Unfortunately, there is no one-size-fits-all pricing model when applying Vested thinking. No generic template or standard spreadsheet can help you get the correct pricing "answer." Establishing the right pricing and incentive mix can be complicated and technical. Yet you do not have to be an accountant, a consultant, or a software engineer to recognize the benefits of a fair pricing structure that rewards innovation. The good news is that developing a pricing model is not a guessing game. Rather, it is a process that parties go through *together* with the goal to create value.

We have found the very best relationships start with both parties sitting on the same side of the table holding transparent, fact-based discussions about the business and desired outcomes. Each party must truly understand the goals and financial drivers of the relationship. We advise companies to resist the urge to use classic negotiation tactics that are not transparent and pit the parties in never-ending battles of trade-offs and concessions. In stark contrast, remember how Procter & Gamble (P&G) viewed itself and its most strategic suppliers as on the same side of the rope, pulling in the same direction.

We also stress the importance of understanding the difference between a "price" and a "pricing model." A transactional approach uses prices. A Vested approach uses a pricing model. Let us look at the difference. A price is an amount you pay for each transaction. You pay $3.25 for your Starbucks grande two-pump vanilla latte. Call center suppliers have a price of $.50 a minute every time an agent picks up the phone and acts as a company's customer service representative.

A pricing model is fundamentally different because it is a *mechanism* used to determine the optimum price between the company and the supplier. In some cases the pricing model consists of nothing more than actual costs, volume targets, and incentives based on estimated value of desired outcomes, such as market share, total cost saving, or customer satisfaction levels. Most pricing models are expressed in a simple spreadsheet; however, some are more like small customized software packages or macro-based Excel® spreadsheets. We use the term *model* because a good pricing protocol enables the parties to manipulate underlying pricing assumptions. This allows the parties to "model" the outputs relative to the input components to determine a fair way to pay for goods and services. A good pricing model with properly crafted incentives enables organizations to go beyond merely mouthing the term *partnership*. Rather, it creates a commercial pricing structure that equitably allocates risks and rewards for the purpose of realizing mutual gains for the duration of the agreement.

Good Vested pricing models have several things in common.

First, all Vested pricing models also typically follow Abraham Maslow's theory of motivation when balancing risk and rewards. Maslow's Hierarchy of Needs theory states that it is vital to meet certain lower needs before addressing higher needs. In the business world, the basic requirement for a service provider is to at least break even in terms of profit on a customer's business. Rather than squeeze margin, a Vested pricing model creates a "safe" operating environment in which a supplier is not going to lose money. Often pricing models strategically guarantee a minimum profit for the supplier in exchange for performing base services. Such models provide everyone peace of mind, knowing the lights will stay on, payroll will be covered, and the equipment or facilities will be properly maintained.

A Vested pricing model usually sees low margins for the base services coupled with incentives that enable suppliers to earn very high margins when they create value by achieving their customers' desired outcomes and solving their business problems. But what constitutes "low base margins" and "very high margins" with incentives? A general rule of thumb is that "low" means below-market margins if the work were bid—often as low as 50 percent of market margin.

For example, if the work was bid out and the "market" margin was 10 percent, a Vested deal might have a 5 percent margin for the base services. Using 10 percent as "market," the rule of thumb in a Vested pricing model allows the supplier to earn two to three times the market margin—or up to 20 to 30 percent profit margins—if it is successful in bringing transformation and innovation to the customer.[1] The Rocky Flats closure project profiled in chapter 4 is a good example. Kaiser-Hill had a base fee set at 3.7 percent (the average margin for Department of Energy contracts was 4.1 percent) with incentives enabling it to earn up to an 11.7 percent profit margin. With incentives clearly in place, Kaiser-Hill earned the maximum bonus payments, resulting in billions of dollars in savings for the Department of Energy.

Another heuristic is not having suppliers assume the full risk of uncontrollables unless the buyer agrees to pay an appropriate and fair risk premium. For example, a facilities management supplier should never be penalized for an increase in energy prices. The rationale is simple. If suppliers are forced to guess at the future of energy prices, they will invariably guess high in order to cover the risk. The quoted price is always inflated for risk, even though the risk may never materialize.

A better way is to accept that the "cost of electricity" is the "cost of electricity" and to develop an incentive for the supplier to mitigate the risk associated with rising costs. For instance, a good incentive would reward a facilities management supplier for designing environmentally sustainable solutions that reduce the kilowatts used per hour. As we discussed earlier, P&G's model is a cost pass-through with Jones Lange LaSalle, with P&G covering the actual cost of electricity. However, incentives are tied to optimization and efficiency—which creates a win-win situation for both parties.

Vested pricing models also recognize that there is a cost to manage the business. Many transaction-based approaches lump the cost of governance into the suppliers' price or, worse, muscular buyers use hard-nosed negotiating tactics to insist that suppliers provide governance for free. Bottom line: It costs money to manage a business. Skimping on governance can create perverse incentives, such as encouraging a supplier to swap out the "A" team with the "C" team after the deal is done. We believe governance costs should be spelled out and that both parties properly resource governance so they do not get the urge to cut corners.

Finally, Vested pricing models often include value exchanges that go well beyond pure financial compensation for suppliers. For instance, suppliers can earn intangible benefits, such as contract extensions, additional business or locations, expanded scope of services, or even references from the customer.

Above all else, Vested pricing models are fair.

Adopting a Vested pricing model requires resisting the temptation and corporate pressures to use procurement muscle and classic negotiation tactics. Instead of aiming at getting the lowest possible *price* from suppliers, the pricing model encourages suppliers to invest in solving a customer's business problems and creating value. This value could take the form of increased market share, increased customer satisfaction, improved time to market—or even reduced costs structures. A good Vested pricing model rewards the supplier for delivering desired outcomes in the form of solutions, not just activities. The better the supplier is at solving the company's problems, the more profit the supplier makes. This approach encourages suppliers to institute innovative and cost-effective methods of performing work to drive down total cost while maintaining or improving service. Properly structured, a Vested pricing model creates an economic exchange in which the more successful the customer, the more successful the supplier.

You might think that moving to a Vested pricing model is a risky venture for a company and its suppliers. Anything new and different involving investment in time, resources, and effort does imply a certain degree of risk. Adrian Gonzales, a well-known analyst in the supply chain sector, offered this advice: "What differentiates the Vested approach are not the risks, which are inherent in any outsourcing relationship, but the potential payoff for both service providers and customers. In other words, the benefits-to-risk ratio is much greater when using a Vested approach. And the risk of remaining at the status quo—in terms of lower profits for suppliers and continued diminishing returns for customers—trumps them all."[2]

Challenging the status quo—shifting away from negotiating a price to jointly developing a fair pricing model with incentives—may seem like a radical idea. But properly structured Vested pricing models can—and do—create paybacks for both parties. One such example is how Microsoft challenged conventional approaches in its award-winning outsourcing agreement with Accenture.

MICROSOFT'S OUTSOURCING PARADOX

A Hackett Group benchmarking effort in 2006 revealed that Microsoft's finance operations were in the fourth quartile, meaning that Microsoft ranked poorly compared to its peers. Taylor Hawes, the area's general manager and controller at the time, pulled together a team of ten Microsoft employees and two full-time consultants to determine how to revamp back-office procure-to-pay processes. The team—called OneFinance—spent a significant amount of time benchmarking potential solutions and brainstorming to decide how best to proceed. It recommended outsourcing Microsoft's accounts payable, buy center, and accounting processes. Microsoft's chairman and founder, Bill Gates, was a proponent of outsourcing non-core activities, and the company had long used that approach to improve its quality and cost structures in non-core functions.[3]

While recognizing that outsourcing might be the answer, Hawes challenged the team to rethink conventional approaches to it. If Microsoft itself invested in transforming the processes to best practices, what would be the advantage of outsourcing? If it outsourced current processes, what motivation would there be for a service provider to make transformational changes? After all, more transactions and headcount meant more revenue for the service provider. Microsoft recognized that it needed an unconventional approach that was not simply about outsourcing the work but about outsourcing the *transformation* of the work.

Hawes explained the strategy. "Microsoft wanted more than simply shifting our 'mess for less'; we wanted an outsourcing business model where we could 'lift and shift' existing operations to a service provider who would then as quickly as possible determine a clear and accurate baseline which they would be expected to improve with Microsoft. The service provider would then be highly compensated for achieving transformational results." Srini Krishna, a management consultant on the team who later joined Microsoft, described the challenge like this: "Our goal was true transformation—and that meant creating a model that went well beyond what is commonly known as gainsharing where a service provider is given a monetary incentive for decreasing cost structures. We needed to develop an approach that would reward our business partner for achieving results that *created value* for our business—not just cost reductions."

It was a radical idea.

But how could Microsoft outsource existing inefficient processes and, at the same time, work with the service provider to transform each process to be more effective and efficient? The OneFinance team spent a significant amount of time laying out existing processes and brainstorming ideas that would help streamline these processes. During those early sessions, Microsoft began to create a vision of what it thought it could achieve. Krishna described the early days as "refreshing." "The early sessions gave the team time and permission to see the bigger picture and understand the flaws with conventional outsourcing approaches."

The team members worked on developing the desired outcomes they hoped to achieve through the outsourcing process. While cutting costs was important, Microsoft—with over $58 billion in sales in 2009—really wanted to create world-class financial processes and infrastructure that would enable it to face the challenges of the twenty-first century. "It would be incorrect to say Microsoft did not think of cost—but what became a core driver for the team was to create an outsourcing model aimed at improving the efficiency and effectiveness of executing Microsoft's financial processes," explained Krishna. The team ultimately created this vision that would drive the outsourcing efforts:

> Best in Class Finance functions, enabled by process standardization, solid internal controls, and effective performance management...achieved by hiring and developing the best people and using integrated applications that showcase Microsoft technology.[4]

With a clear vision as the foundation, the team set out to find an outsource partner that would help Microsoft turn vision into reality as quickly as possible.

WIIFWE

History has consequences. One of the key challenges Microsoft faced was its reputation; it had long been known in the marketplace as the proverbial 800-pound gorilla. Krishna explained the problem. "Microsoft was used to winning—but they had the wrong definition for winning. We needed to change our thinking that win-win didn't mean that Microsoft could win twice." In other words, instead of thinking about What's In It For Me (WIIFMe), it was time to think about What's In It For We (WIIFWe).

Microsoft had effectively used what Nobel Prize–winning economist Dr. Oliver Williamson called a classic "muscular" approach in the marketplace. "Muscular buyers not only use their suppliers, but they often 'use up' their suppliers and discard them. The muscular approach to outsourcing of goods and services is myopic and inefficient."[5] Krishna—a formally educated economist—knew that such an approach would not work if Microsoft wanted to get outsource providers to invest heavily in improving its business. The team needed to develop a contract and pricing model that created mutual advantages for both parties. The more successful the service provider, the more successful Microsoft would be.

FROM THEORY TO STRATEGY

Pricing the work fairly became the topic of many philosophical debates among the OneFinance team. Various approaches about how to fairly compensate potential service providers were discussed. Not surprisingly, the team faced many complex challenges inherited from more than two decades of breakneck global growth in Microsoft's businesses. Rapid growth across geographies and individual business lines in an entrepreneurial work environment had left a decentralized finance organization with disparate processes and systems. The organization focused on growing business and tracking market trends; it paid little effort to tracking the efficiency and effectiveness of finance operations. Further, finance operations were always part of the general overhead with no associated service levels or expectations.

Henric Häggquist, a former controller of the Nordic region for Microsoft, was on the OneFinance team early on. "Decentralized subsidiaries encouraged controllers to achieve local optimization rather than global efficiencies in the processes. This meant Microsoft had a very limited ability to identify their true cost structure. This became clear early in the process when the team identified approximately 140 different systems and field applications. The cost to manage the systems was mostly hidden in the field and was not systematically captured. For example, many subsidiaries maintained locally developed tools to support finance processes. The time and effort to maintain a plethora of systems was burdened in headcount and other 'hidden administrative costs,' but not visible at the global level. By quickly lifting and shifting work to their potential service provider, Microsoft could effectively begin with a clean slate while at the same time obtain a true baseline of all of the costs."

But consultant Krishna knew unknowns and variability in Microsoft's business would spell trouble for a service provider. "Unknowns and variability would increase risks and lead to a 'supernormal' risk premium over and above the 'normal' business risks. This was an important concept and one that Dr. Oliver Williamson stressed many years ago in his Nobel Prize–winning work on transaction cost economics. Microsoft discovered through their discussions what Dr. Williamson had written about for several years: Any potential service provider would have to raise their price if they were forced to contract for 'unknowns.'"

The OneFinance team knew that its vision of transforming Microsoft's back-office finance processes would lie in getting the economics right in the pricing model. It would be imperative to design a pricing model aimed at compensating a service provider for achieving transformational results, not simply performing base services. During early discussions, it was clear that Accenture, a global management consulting, technology services, and outsourcing company, also preferred a commercial model in which incentives were aligned. Accenture had strong marketplace experiences where the best engagements were set up in a Vested manner. After much deliberation, the parties agreed on a strategy to use a hybrid approach that included four building blocks. The building blocks, when combined, created an overall pricing model base that would not only be fair but would provide significant incentives to drive productivity and transformation efforts. The building blocks were:

1. *Base Services.* The base services represented the core of the work to be performed. This was work that had to be performed consistently during the contract duration—such as paying invoices or maintaining basic accounting functions that were vital to the business. The repetitive and stable nature of this work enabled the parties to use a fixed fee based on volume bands and an assumed productivity increase (discussed later) and would have the lowest margin for the potential service provider.

2. *Other Services.* From the outset, the parties knew they would not be able to define all of the future unknown work in the base services. Often known as "scope creep" in the industry, this provision for "other services" allowed parties to agree on how to price future unknown work in an efficient manner. Ultimately this work was priced based on an agreed-upon rate card using predefined job roles and local rates.

3. *Infrastructure/Governance.* Managing a business is not free. The OneFinance team knew it would be imperative to have proper staffing levels to get—and retain—the service provider's "A" team, consisting of highly qualified people. Thus, the pricing model design called for separating out the cost of governance to ensure Microsoft and the service provider placed proper emphasis on governance.

4. *Transformation.* The last building block would incentivize transformation. By design, Microsoft wanted to create a formal mechanism that would significantly reward a potential service provider for investing in successful transformation initiatives.

With the foundational building blocks in place, Microsoft moved forward to select a service provider that would not only embrace the challenge of transforming Microsoft's back-office procure-to-pay processes but would also welcome its pricing model with its significant risk and reward elements. Accenture was one of two finalists, and it embraced the concept of having a pricing model where it had skin in the game. "We were excited about the concept of creating a shared risk–shared reward pricing model where Accenture had a true vested interest in Microsoft's success," explained Gil Wootton, executive partner for the Microsoft relationship. "Accenture has the A+ brainpower and commitment to deliver on innovative solutions like what Microsoft was asking for. An innovative pricing model would enable Accenture to have highly competitive rates for the overall base services while still allowing us to earn higher margin through incentives pending we could deliver on the promise of transformation. Pricing the business with such a large percentage of our margin at risk, alongside our ability to control how the work is delivered, meant Accenture would be in solid alignment with Microsoft's goals."

Microsoft selected Accenture as the preferred provider, and the companies set out to perfect the pricing model to mirror Microsoft's desired outcomes to drive transformation.

PERFECTING THE PRICING MODEL

Global Model with Local Adjustments

From a pricing perspective, the scope of countries in the contract presented unique challenges. Although the overall objective of having a single global pricing model was paramount, it was equally critical to recognize the fact that differences in language and time zones had to be factored into the model. For example, Accenture would need to hire English-speaking employees, and these resources would have to be different for Australia and the United Kingdom because, despite a common language, the resources operated in different time zones. Similarly, a Croatian and a Slovenian resource with the same accounts payable skills might operate from the same time zone but with entirely different perspectives of resource deployment and their associated costs. Finally, as Microsoft business grew at different rates in different countries, the model had to support varying resource requirements that reflected the time zones and languages so that Accenture could continue to support contracted service levels.

To allow for these differences, the pricing model classified all in-scope countries into groups based on process skills (accounts payable, record and buy center), time zone, and language. This approach ensured a fair price for each resource in the various markets.

Volume Banding Philosophy—Flexibility, Leverage, and Risk Mitigation

Volume fluctuations were one of the few certainties that faced the OneFinance team. Volumes could (and likely would) go up and potentially could even go down. The commercial structure had to be adaptive to absorb these fluctuations and adjust service charges appropriately without requiring contract discussions and negotiations.

Microsoft and Accenture agreed to a volume banding philosophy to allow flexibility in the model. The volume banding philosophy enabled Microsoft and Accenture to establish a minimum fee that it would pay Accenture for base services, known as the "floor." The rationale was simple: The floor enabled Accenture to cover its fixed costs. Next, pricing would adjust automatically within "volume bands" as Microsoft's volume fluctuated. The volume banding concept addressed volume uncertainties by enabling management of fixed and variable costs. An increase in volumes was at a discounted rate because additional volumes did not result in increased fixed costs (i.e., additional management, governance layer, or infrastructure [seating]). The existing fixed costs could absorb certain additional variable costs; volume increases beyond predetermined thresholds led to repricing based on an established rate card as volume increased. The model worked the same way if volumes declined from the baselines, as volumes below the "floor" would mean Microsoft would pay higher rates in those volume bands.

Volume banding allowed the model to adjust to changing business conditions yet still enabled both companies to meet their commercial objectives by mitigating risks. For Accenture, the minimum floor of guaranteed volumes protected its revenue up to a point from declines in transaction volumes. Likewise, Microsoft was protected against unplanned increases in charges due to unprecedented growth in volume.

Fee at Risk—An Incentive to Drive Continuous Improvement

A second key element of the pricing model was the use of a fee-at-risk strategy whereby Accenture would risk part of its fees against committed productivity gains. Microsoft wanted to ensure that Accenture was using its expertise to drive productivity improvements that would lower Microsoft's overall cost of the contract. Three distinct elements—annual productivity gains, annual volume absorption and dead-band volume absorption are discussed in the sections that follow. Together the elements yielded a combination of guaranteed benefits for Microsoft. The model also allowed Accenture to improve its financials when it exceeded the guaranteed benefit level for Microsoft.

Annual Productivity Gains

Both sides accepted the basic principle that repetitive, ongoing work leads to natural productivity increases. Following this principle, Accenture committed to delivering productivity benefits on the base services over the life of the contract. Accenture is the industry leader in finance and accounting outsourcing and has significant experience with the specific areas of focus for Microsoft. This gave both companies confidence that the productivity benefits were achievable. The concept of a productivity index was critical in delivering productivity gains. The index measured the productivity of each Accenture resource for each process area every year of the contract (transaction volume per full-time equivalent [FTE]). It was assumed that at the point of transition the productivity levels would be exactly the same for the resources of both companies. This equivalence was achieved by transferring to Accenture on a 1:1 basis the headcount performing the work within Microsoft. For example, if five FTEs were performing the scope of work being transferred within the Microsoft subsidiary, Accenture would create five positions in its delivery center for the same volume of work at the point of transition of services. This method helped set a common baseline and a starting point to measure productivity.

Following this, Accenture would deliver a guaranteed percentage increase in productivity each year of the contract. The increased productivity was translated into reduced service fees for base services each contract year.

Volume Absorption

A second component of the fee-at-risk strategy was the annual volume absorption by Accenture. Microsoft and Accenture set a baseline annual volume at the point of the transfer of operations. From that point forward, Accenture agreed to absorb a maximum of 6 percent growth in transaction volumes each contract year. In other words, Accenture would be responsible for achieving productivity goals that would meet or exceed the 6 percent target, or it would face a reduction in profit margins.

Dead-Band Intra-Year Volume Variations

Both Microsoft and Accenture knew that natural volume variations occur in the course of business. Thus, they created the concept of a dead band to account for natural intra-year volume variations. The annual volume absorption threshold already described, actual or up to a maximum of 6 percent of the prior year, set the baseline for the year. On this baseline, Accenture would not charge additional service fees for volume increases within a 5 percent dead band (buffer).

Benefits

The fee-at-risk approach offered several benefits, most notably guaranteed productivity gains. Such a guarantee enabled Microsoft to feel more comfortable with a seven-year, long-term contract with Accenture. Accenture accepted the risk because, if it beat the productivity assumptions, it could keep the extra profits or reinvest in the overall relationship. The long-term contract also gave Accenture confidence to invest time and resources to improve the processes. Instead of spending time rebidding the work, both parties had fruitful and meaningful discussions each year to identify transformation projects to implement.

A Value-Share Incentive Structure to Drive Transformational Behaviors

The OneFinance team members knew that a partnership with Accenture could open up a door to take them beyond what they could achieve by themselves. The key would lie in getting the economics right to compensate Accenture for achieving transformational results and allow for bringing in expertise from Accenture's consulting and information technology practices. Tim McBride explains the logic behind Microsoft's approach for incentivizing Accenture for transformation. "The OneFinance team challenged us to develop a breakthrough approach to 'gainshare' that would ensure transformation was achieved in an environment of partnership and trust. The team researched the strengths and weaknesses of existing approaches and ultimately developed a simple mathematical model to reward Accenture for successful transformation initiatives." The approach included four basic philosophies:

1. Shared intent
2. Tangible returns
3. Up-front agreement on fair share
4. Simplicity

Shared Intent

Both companies knew that they could achieve transformational results only in partnership. This meant that who brings an idea to the table is irrelevant. For Microsoft, the opportunity gain of the financial benefits was immense even after it shared a portion with Accenture. Sharing made sense; the benefit was not there otherwise. Krishna explained: "Some might call it greed, but in this instance greed is good. The possibility of creating more than what one already had in itself creates a significant desire to embark on this journey. The contract clearly and unequivocally articulated the joint intent to collaborate on a transformation program integral to the outsourcing arrangement and taking Microsoft's finance processes to world-class levels as measured by a third-party benchmark."

Tangible Returns

The shared vision was crucial to ensure that both parties were aligned, but the intent had to be backed by a financial model that provided commercial justification for both sides to continue investing and collaborating in the transformation journey. Both parties knew that to actually implement transformation initiatives, each company would have to be incentivized to go beyond simply performing the base services. The other key element to success was establishing a governance structure for managing the gain-share model.

The companies believed that focusing on implementing financially viable projects—transformation initiatives—would bring tangible returns on investment. Tim McBride explained: "The organizations viewed transformational incentives with the philosophy that together both sides were creating a bigger pie— unlocking financial value that was not being realized by either party previously. As such, incentives would be paid for successful implementation of transformation projects when value—or return on investments—was realized. Increasing the size of the pie was fundamental to enhancing the spirit of partnership. Carving the existing pie differently would only lead to conflict between the two sides."

Up-front Agreement on Fair Share

As the parties worked through the details of the pricing model, Accenture raised a critical concern: "A widespread problem of gainsharing is that clients struggled when it comes time to writing the incentives check," explained Patricia Humphrey, the Accenture partner for Microsoft's Business Process Outsourcing Delivery at Microsoft. "We had found that gainsharing could almost be a curse because if Accenture was highly successful, the incentive bonus could get large and companies often would create excuses why they should not do a full payout. We knew it was critical to get the transformation incentive component of the pricing model right since we would be making significant investments unique to the Microsoft business that could not be leveraged across other clients."

Krishna sympathized with Accenture. "Transformation is about creating value and expanding the pie. Everyone is happy when transformation projects are successful. But then reality sets in when it's time to write the incentive check to the service provider for their fair share. All too often people end up fighting over just what is their 'fair share.' Service providers get gun-shy about doing transformation projects, and you end up not much further ahead than when you started. We were adamant that we wanted to formally define and develop contractual mechanisms that would make Accenture feel comfortable that if they made smart investments that created value, they would get their fair share." In short, defining the fair share approach enabled Accenture to be confident about investing in a relationship with Microsoft. If Accenture was successful, it would be rewarded with additional margin, even though the overall revenue might be reduced.

The parties jointly developed a simple mathematical model to compute the fair share of each transformation initiative. Using that model, each company can estimate its fair share of project returns up front based on a projected business case. Accenture's share of benefits is computed to include:

- Implementation cost
- Compensation for profit margin on the revenue (represented by the benefits) lost due to project implementation
- Transformation incentive percentage (agreed up front)

Simplicity

Krishna explained the importance of having a simple approach for managing gainsharing: "Most transformation gainshare programs become unique to a type of project. So over the life of a program, you wind up developing individual models for individual projects to meet the need for each project. We explicitly did not want this to be the case with OneFinance. We strove to have *one* model that could work across all types of transformation projects." This simplicity enables the parties to manage the payout schemes easily and can outlive the individuals involved in the original agreement.

Accenture is no longer worried about the gainshare component of the OneFinance pricing model, stated Andrew Cheung, the Accenture partner responsible the OneFinance. "You don't need a Ph.D. in finance to make it work. The beauty is it is simple yet robust enough to work across all of the transformation projects. We've had the model in place since we started in February 2007, and it has never failed us. We know our fair share. It is simple. It just works. I have no hesitation to make heavy investments in Microsoft because we've proven the pricing model works—again and again."

Häggquist, who went on to become the senior director of Microsoft's finance operations in charge of the Accenture relationship, was quick to point out that the incentive structure has worked very well. "The OneFinance's team gut was right. Aligning incentives to the success of transformation initiatives would highly motivate Accenture. The more successful Accenture made Microsoft, the more successful they themselves would be. Our simple yet robust approach works. During the first twenty-seven months, Microsoft was able to achieve 11 transformation projects that have resulted in over $30 million in value for Microsoft." In fact, Microsoft began seeing quantifiable benefits from the projects six short months after its initial investment.

WAS IT A GOOD DEAL?

But how do you know you got a good deal? This question bothered the Microsoft OneFinance team. Henric Häggquist, a former controller, explained the problem: "Most companies look at outsourcing from purely a contract and cost perspective. In addition, costs often get allocated as 'corporate overheads' and 'corporate budgets' and result in difficulty determining value for costs." Krishna agreed. "Treating outsourcing as a contract with allocations leads to what economists call the 'free rider problem.' A lack of transparency and accountability often gives business units or subsidiaries the attitude of 'someone in corporate' pays for services and is in control. In short, it does not give the business units and users of the service any incentive to drive costs down or benefits up."

To address the free rider problem, the Microsoft team decided to create mechanisms to treat the Accenture outsourcing relationship like a business, not a contract. This meant creating a profit and loss statement and a complete balanced scorecard for OneFinance. Krishna and his fellow teammates set out to establish a comprehensive internal controls process for managing Microsoft's finance operations that would help them prove they were getting a good return on their investment. The two companies decided to develop a financial statement model to reflect revenue, costs, and savings to ensure that finance operations retained accountability for the overall program. Using a profit and loss statement to document outsourcing costs would shift subsidiaries from passive bystanders to having skin in the game. Rather than being regarded as a simple cost burden, subsidiaries would actively approve transformation initiatives that would generate a return on investment. Together, the control mechanisms would drive the right behaviors within Microsoft. The details of the mechanics are outlined next.

Estimating Revenue

The first part of the OneFinance internal financial statement was the revenue. Revenue was calculated from two sources: transaction revenue and governance revenue.

Transactions are calculated by estimating the costs charged to subsidiaries for consuming the services provided through the program. To ensure fairness, the team started with the operations, costs, and volume of work the subsidiaries were using when the services transitioned to Accenture. This formed the baseline cost and volume for the subsidiaries. Since the transition involved a one-to-one transfer of headcount to Accenture, this reflected the fair value of the cost of service for each subsidiary; it was what they would have incurred if they had performed the work in house.

Based on the volume of work being transitioned, the headcount cost was translated into a transaction cost that was used to compute future costs of the subsidiary in the outsourced model. For instance, if the baseline transaction cost was $1.08 per transaction, an annual consumption of 100 transactions would entail an annual charge-back of $108 to the subsidiary. These transactions became one of the two components of the revenue that would be reflected in the internal financial statement. It enabled the subsidiaries to see the direct costs associated with the volume of work they consumed. The transaction cost model worked for accounts payable and buy center services; due to its idiosyncrasies, the records department continued to follow the resource-based pricing model.

The second source of revenue came from a charge for managing—or governing—the program. The team recognized that the cost to the subsidiary had to include the cost of governance. In an insourced model, each subsidiary bears a similar cost, the cost of managing operations, although that cost is buried in corporate overhead. This model provided visibility into the cost of governance, which led to accountability for efficient governance within finance operations.

A specific line item in the budget reflected a subsidiary's consumption of services and cost of governance. Thus, subsidiaries could clearly understand the costs associated with the services they were receiving.

Cost of the Delivery Model

The cost component of the internal financial statement was the outsourcing fees charged by Accenture.

Profit or Savings of the Delivery Model

The difference between the revenue received from the subsidiaries and the costs paid to Accenture reflected the profits from the outsourced model. In essence, these were bottom-line savings associated with the outsourced program. The profits were reported each month to the field leadership and transferred to the subsidiaries each year. In that sense, finance operations became a zero-budget organization where all costs and revenue belonged to the ultimate customer, the field organization. At the end of the year, field organizations could decide on the best way to utilize the profits from their efforts.

Savings generated from transformation projects added to the overall profits of the program and funded additional projects. With agreement from the field leadership team, savings from transformation projects were plowed back into the program to fund new initiatives. For example, in 2010 the field organizations directed the OneFinance team to invest in electronic invoicing as a project that would drive additional efficiencies.

Reinvestment of savings meant that new initiatives did not lead to further budget requests, and the overall program became self-funding.

Benefits of This Approach

The primary benefit of this approach was transparency. Under the program, the end customers—the subsidiaries—could directly see that their dollars were buying not just transactional service delivery but program governance where they could see actual performance improvements. The second benefit was the elimination of the free rider problem. Knowing the cost of their demands for additional services changed the way subsidiaries interacted with finance operations. Although they could ask for additional services, it came with a cost to them.

Third, the model enabled Microsoft and Accenture to validate that savings from transformation projects were actualized profits. Reporting on the savings and using them to drive the transformation agenda forward created a disciplined approach to the entire process. "Accenture values the innovative model; it allows us to bring more and more creative ideas to the table," said Joseph Wright, the partner responsible for transformation at Microsoft's finance organization.

There was another, unintended benefit. Quite often in ousourcing contracts, the well-intentioned desire to please the customer—in this case, the subsidiaries—leads to a service provider saying yes to extra work. This is often referred to as "scope creep."

The downside is that these extra services—while desired and asked for—can significantly increase costs. As such, they often are the source of disagreements when it comes time to pay the bill. Under the OneFinance pricing model, Accenture had clear instructions on how to manage subsidiaries' requests for additional services. Such requests had to go through formal contract change order processes that ensured all internal expectations were managed and buy-in is obtained before any change is implemented. The contract included a formal way for Accenture to push back on scope creep.

BUT IS IT A GOOD DEAL FOR ACCENTURE?

It is important to remember that a Vested approach is about mutual advantage. Both parties win. Many asked whether Accenture was getting a good deal. Gil Wootton smiled when he talked about Accenture's relationship with Microsoft. "While margins were minimal on the base book of work, the pricing model and seven-year contract enabled Accenture to use its expertise and insight to take cost out of the baseline quickly, resulting in profit margins above market rates. Accenture also shares in the value of the transformation projects.... Typical outsourcing arrangements have poor profitability in the early stages; the transformation agenda with Microsoft OneFinance allowed us to be more profitable in the first two years than when we work on a headcount basis."

But the rewards go beyond transformation gainsharing for achieving transformation. Based on its success, Accenture has been rewarded with additional work. Microsoft added the accounts payable and buy center operations from its Fargo location and extended the contract with Accenture by four years. What started out as a $185 million contract is today valued at $330 million and runs through 2018. Accenture has a future revenue stream as part of a long-term contract that most service providers would envy. The long-term contract reduces Accenture's cost to serve over the life of the contract because it does not have to bid for the work on a regular basis, as it does for most clients who suffer from the bid-and-transition syndrome of constantly testing market prices.

But probably the best benefits for Accenture are intangible. "The flexible agreement has allowed Accenture to be a part of key transformational projects for Microsoft—an enviable position in the marketplace. Over the course of the five-year program, Accenture has developed a credential in terms of scope of service, geographic spread, and languages being covered. Our work with Microsoft continues to position Accenture very strongly in the finance and accounting marketplace," said Mike Salvino, group chief executive for business process outsourcing at Accenture. "Microsoft OneFinance is one of the most innovative relationships we have in the marketplace and has become a foundation for how we think about driving future generations of BPO [Business Process Outsourcing]."

VESTED FOR SUCCESS

The OneFinance team set out to create a different kind of outsourcing model. From the early days of brainstorming ideas to the inking of the contract in February 2007, the team challenged conventional approaches to outsourcing that would transform Microsoft's back-office procure-to-pay processes. The bet is paying off. Microsoft's strategic outsourcing relationship began to see paybacks after the first six months.

Within the first two years, the team had reduced the number of systems used to manage finance operations from 140 to less than 40 and achieved 99.5 percent operational service levels. By year 5, the Microsoft-Accenture duo had achieved over 75 percent standardization across all processes, yielding productivity gains of 18 percent and an additional costs savings of $63 million for Microsoft. But the best result comes from getting to sleep at night. Together Microsoft and Accenture have conquered compliance. They increased Sarbanes-Oxley compliance from just 15 large subsidiaries to all 96 subsidiaries within the first two years of the contract and were proud to report zero unremediated Sarbanes-Oxley 404/302 audit control deficiencies.[6]

Microsoft and Accenture are now moving on to more strategic challenges, such as the joint development of procure-to-pay tools on Microsoft's Dynamics platform that are being rolled out internally. The success of Dynamics offers significant future revenue potential for Microsoft products. Accenture benefits from including Microsoft's new Dynamics tools in its rapidly expanding Business Process Outsourcing service offering.

The two companies have been so successful that they are widely lauded for ingenuity as well as exceptional performance. Among the many awards they have won are the Outsourcing Center's Most Strategic Outsourcing Contract (2008), the Shared Services Outsourcing Network's Best Mature Outsourced Service Delivery Operation (2010), and the International Association for Outsourcing Professionals' Global Excellence in Outsourcing (GEO) for Innovation in Outsourcing (2011), and Shared Services Outsource Network's Award for Excellence in customer service in Asia.

Häggquist was quick to point out that "the awards are nice, but the best award for the OneFinance team is knowing that we are achieving our aggressive goals." He also insisted that Microsoft could not be successful without Accenture. In fact, he emphasized the importance of thinking and acting in the spirit of together—in the spirit of WIIFWe—in an email to the entire OneFinance team after winning a recent award:

> So why do we get these awards??
> I say it is because of TOGETHER.
> We face all things TOGETHER.

We win TOGETHER.

We face difficulties TOGETHER.

We never go YOU against US.

We have all seen what that leads to...

I couldn't be more proud than I am right now.

Proud TOGETHER with all of you!!!

Thanks for the hard work you all do!!!!!

—Henric Häggquist

Sr. Director, OneFinance

"We cannot be more proud of the relationship we have established with the Microsoft OneFinance team. The TOGETHER-based relationship permeates our behavior," said Gil Wootton. "We know we have to earn this level of relationship confidence every day. OneFinance will continue to be a highlight of many Accenture careers."

The OneFinance contract is a shining example of what a Vested relationship should be. Microsoft believes it is on the path to achieve what it set out to achieve, but it is doing so with the help of a business partner. Both Microsoft and Accenture are on the same journey, *working together* to drive out waste and create world-class financial processes and an infrastructure to run Microsoft's finance operations.

WHAT'S NEXT?

The OneFinance team is not resting on its laurels. In the spirit of transformation, the team continues to reinvent itself and push to newer heights. The Microsoft/Accenture team just embarked on a joint, three-year strategic plan that resulted in a host of new goals and objectives that will challenge the team to reach even higher achievements. Its new aim is to win recognition for excellence in a world-class controls and compliance process.

Mike Simms, Microsoft's chief outsourcing officer, offered a last piece of advice: "We have learned that applying a Vested philosophy requires a cultural change in how we will need to work with our service providers. For Microsoft, this means exploring the Vested approach one program and one service provider at a time—working to build trust with our supply base and business units that outsource to understand that there really is a better way. The OneFinance program has given us a powerful model we can use with other strategic outsourcing programs."

6

MCDONALD'S SECRET SAUCE FOR SUPPLY CHAIN SUCCESS

None of us is as good as all of us.

—*Ray Kroc*

RULE #5: INSIGHT VERSUS OVERSIGHT GOVERNANCE

Last but not least. Governance may be the last of the Vested Five Rules, but it is perhaps the most important. Following the first four rules helps you get to a good agreement—but you have to manage it. If you do not manage it well, the consequences are costly. In fact, leading industry research found that poor governance can erode up to 90 percent of anticipated value.[1]

This is often called "value erosion" or "savings leakage" and is a pressing problem for companies.

One key reason business relationships are so hard to manage is because the very nature of business relationships is fluid. Although many deals are often struck on a handshake, most end with lawyers documenting details that become out of date after the contract is signed because assumptions change and markets are dynamic. Simply put, rigid contractual documents that do not embrace the fact that "business happens" can create frustration or, worse, lawsuits.

According to legal scholar Ian MacNeil, "Somewhere along the line of increasing duration and complexity [the agreement] escapes the traditional legal model."[2] MacNeil's work points to a key reason why traditional legal theory is not adequate in today's business environment: "Classical law views cooperation as being 'of little interest' and external to the agreement. This argues for an agreement framework that encourages cooperation and dialogue." MacNeil taught that agreements can be "governed efficiently only if the parties adopt a consciously cooperative attitude."[3] Dr. Oliver E. Williamson, the Nobel laureate economist, also contributed to this theme, writing that "all complex agreements will be incomplete—there will be gaps, errors, omissions and the like."[4]

What can business and legal communities do if a contract or agreement is incomplete due to the dynamic nature of business? According to Williamson, an agreement between organizations should be a flexible framework and a process for understanding the relationship between the parties. Building flexibility into agreements prevents what he called "maladaptations." A maladaptation is something designed into the agreement that subsequently becomes more harmful than helpful.

How then do you govern a process that is vague, changing, and incomplete? How do you gain insight in a relationship to see potential opportunities—and challenges—before they become harmful? Governance makes the difference between success and failure.

A good governance structure increases understanding of the business by all parties and helps them to make changes that help both parties take smart actions. A Vested governance framework uses a relationship management structure and joint processes as control mechanisms to encourage the organizations to make ethical, proactive changes for the mutual benefit of all the parties.[5] Good governance is a joint process in which parties work together to achieve clearly defined and measurable outcomes. Good governance enables companies to avoid maladaptations.

A flexible agreement addresses the dynamic nature of business head-on by crafting mechanisms that cope with unanticipated disturbances as they arise. A good governance structure includes mechanisms to enable the parties in a relationship to adapt to, and achieve, business changes—the mechanisms, in effect, help keep the parties aligned and continually working toward desired outcomes. The desired outcomes are, in essence, the beacon, the governance structure mechanism that allows the parties to stop and redirect their efforts when market conditions change or assumptions are inaccurate.

A good governance structure creates an environment and mechanisms for developing improved business insight and embraces proactive changes that can help companies achieve their desired outcomes.

Three elements are needed to craft a Vested governance structure that provides insight, not just oversight. The flexible framework can be used for all types of business arrangements—from the simplest to the most complex. Organizations can tailor the framework to suit their needs rather than guess what else to add.

The three elements in a Vested governance framework include:

1. *Relationship management.* The relationship management structure formulates and supports joint policies that emphasize the importance of building collaborative working relationships, attitudes, and behaviors. The structure is flexible and provides top-to-bottom insights about what

is happening with the parties' desired outcomes as well as the relationship between the parties.

2. *Transformation management.* Vested agreements are transformative because in the Vested environment, change is both desirable and expected. Transformation management supports the transition from old to new as well as improvement of end-to-end business processes. The focus is on mutual accountability for attaining desired outcomes and the creation of an ecosystem that rewards innovation and a culture of continuous improvement.

3. *Exit management.* The future is unknown. Even the best plans can fail, and events will change the business environment. An exit management strategy provides procedures to handle these unknowns.[6]

Applying effective governance in a business relationship maximizes the potential for a successful partnership. Effective governance also provides a framework for decision making, renegotiation, and modification as circumstances change.

But just how does McDonald's structure a governance framework that provides insight and has the power to align suppliers so tightly, they are excited about making investments not only for their own benefit but for McDonald's? And how does it inspire suppliers to reach for uncompromising levels of quality and safety? McDonald's secret sauce for governance is worth delving into.

A SYSTEM TO BE RECKONED WITH

It was a simple decision.

From the beginning, founder Ray Kroc decided to use an outsourced model for his operations. He did not have the funds he needed to build his own vertical supply chain. But lack of funds was only part of Kroc's reason for wanting to outsource.

He was also disgusted with the franchising systems in the United States at the time, as they were known for taking advantage of owner/operators and accepting kickbacks from suppliers.[7] He also knew that existing franchises were woefully lacking in consistency in terms of food quality, preparation, and handling. Kroc envisioned a better way, one where his company—McDonald's— would create an alliance with restaurant owner/operators and suppliers that operated with long-term thinking based on trust and transparency. Kroc surrounded McDonald's with suppliers who were entrepreneurs and were not hesitant to try new things and invest in the McDonald's System. Kroc formed partnerships with owner/operators and suppliers so solid—so dependable, that they became known as the "System." The System promise? When McDonald's succeeds, they will succeed. In the System, everyone succeeds.

In 1955, it was a radical idea.

That was over a half a century ago, and today McDonald's System is a force to be reckoned with. Kroc created true supplier partnerships that have become a competitive advantage for McDonald's supply chain. Although Ray Kroc has passed on, his legacy is larger than life as he embedded a culture that institutionalized the "System First" philosophy in the DNA of McDonald's and its suppliers.

"This philosophy is often described as a three-legged stool. One of the legs is McDonald's employees, a second leg is the owner/operators that run the restaurants, and the third leg is McDonald's supplier partners. The stool is only as strong as the three legs. This means that the company employees...the franchise owner/operators...and the suppliers each support the weight of McDonald's equally. As Ray Kroc was fond of saying, In business for yourself, but not by yourself."[8]

McDonald's outsourced supply chain model gives suppliers a seat at the table. That seat, however, comes with the expectation that they will create a competitive advantage for McDonald's. The

System is based on the principle of creating long-term wealth and competitive advantage for all three legs of the stool. This is accomplished through mitigating costs, preventing safety issues, and producing quality and innovative products that delight customers in a uniquely McDonald's way. The result is increased customer value, better brand health, and stronger business performance.

Ray Kroc established a precedent of trust, loyalty, and fairness with suppliers that motivates them to invest in McDonald's business—creating a marketplace advantage in key business drivers such as cleanliness, quality, value, assured supply, safety, and all-in-all being better, not just bigger. What is surprising is that McDonald's suppliers invest in McDonald's business without formal contracts. That's right. McDonald's does business with strategic suppliers based on the commitment of an old-fashioned handshake. Kroc believed that as long as both McDonald's and the suppliers stay loyal to their long-term "System First" thinking, a trusting handshake was all that was needed. The flexibility of a handshake agreement to principles rather than detailed SLAs (service-level agreements) allows McDonald's to address dynamic changes in the market and business needs as they occur.

Francesca DeBiase, McDonald's vice president of strategic sourcing, Worldwide Supply Chain Management, explained the rationale for handshake deals. "Many of our strategic suppliers have been working with McDonald's for years, even decades. They know that we base our partnerships on mutual trust, respect, and financial success. Over the years, our actions and behaviors have shown our suppliers that we conduct business with a high level of integrity. This allows us to operate with a handshake agreement."[9]

McDonald's consistent treatment of suppliers elicits positive and sometimes amazing responses. Pete Richter, president of the Global McDonald's business unit for Cargill[10] and chair of the U.S. Supplier Advisory Council, explained how a long-term relationship founded on high degrees of trust impacts Cargill's interaction. "The trust and confidence in the future means we shift 90% of our resources to driving innovation, quality, supply chain optimization, and investing in future growth initiatives. This takes trust on both sides of the table; once established, it creates amazing leverage vs. the traditional arm's length RFP type approach."[11]

Indeed, suppliers who help McDonald's succeed thrive themselves by building their own business in ways they did not think possible. Simply put, McDonald's and its suppliers have a Vested interest in helping each other succeed. And it all started with a vision and philosophy that said, "None of us is as good as all of us."

It is hard to argue that Ray Kroc's insistence on the What's-In-It-For-We (WIIFWe) approach created the world's most powerful restaurant business and supply chain. The results are staggering. By 2012, Kroc's System has expanded to over 100 countries and 33,000 restaurants serving more than 68 million customers a day. McDonald's sets the standards in food quality, safety, and consistency. It is on the top of the charts in *Fortune*, *Forbes*, and *Bloomberg* rankings for a gamut of achievements, including brands, respect, stock value, leadership, and sustainability. Indeed, McDonald's does have a secret sauce when it comes to dealing with suppliers. But how has McDonald's sustained the culture for over 50 years, especially since Ray Kroc's death in 1984?

One answer is the insight governance structure that builds in innovation and transformation. McDonald's transcends simply managing suppliers to managing the business strategically with suppliers. It relies on the long-term System First philosophy to stay ahead of dynamic market conditions and to never compromise McDonald's commitment to quality and food safety.

PLANNING TO WIN

In 2003, McDonald's senior leadership created a customer-focused long-term strategy called the "Plan to Win." It concentrates on being better, not just bigger, and provides a common framework for global business while still allowing for local adaptation. And, above all else, it creates even more of a competitive advantage.

The Plan to Win is a strategic blueprint that helps all parties in the System focus on the core drivers of McDonald's business. The objective is to keep the McDonald's brand relevant. The Plan to Win outlines four key supply chain priorities providing value for the McDonald's System and ultimately ending with customers eating at McDonald's. The priorities are:

1. Attract more customers.
2. Convince customers to purchase more often.
3. Increase brand loyalty.
4. Become more profitable.

In other words, more customers, more often, more brand loyalty, more profitability: These are the bottom-line goals for brand success.

The Plan to Win is the driving force behind all McDonald's actions and strategies, and it is a significant factor in increasingly effective supply chain initiatives. McDonald's has always had strong supplier partnerships, but it strengthened strategic relationships by creating a formal alignment process with the Plan to Win. In true McDonald's fashion, the company is transparent about sharing its Plan to Win openly with suppliers. In fact, McDonald's not only shares the plan; it expects suppliers to develop both annual business plans and long-term strategic plans that align with the plan.

Doing a joint Plan to Win and creating alignment is easier said than done. That is why McDonald's tapped Gary Johnson, senior director of the Worldwide Supply Chain, to lead a joint McDonald's/ supplier team to document and describe desired behaviors—known as the Value of Supply Chain. Johnson explained: "While we had a legacy of how we behaved, we did not have a formal written document that codified our approach. We wanted both McDonald's and our suppliers to understand how behaviors provide a competitive advantage to the System. And behaviors start with us. Just by having suppliers have a seat at the table, McDonald's demonstrates the importance of how McDonald's/supplier interaction are a critical are of discussion."[12]

Zoran Rancic, McDonald's supply chain director (agriculture products) for Asia, continued, "It is our goal to have both McDonald's and the supplier sitting shoulder to shoulder on the same side of the table working to make the best possible decisions for the System. This allows us to see the bigger picture with much more clarity. For example, food commodity markets create a challenge for our producers. Having a Plan to Win and Value of Supply Chain behaviors as guides, we work with suppliers to optimize System First supply chain decisions. This process helps our suppliers make smart investments that yield the best benefits for everyone."[13]

This deep-seated trust and inclusion wins the hearts and minds of suppliers like Midd McManus, Dean Foods' vice president of the McDonald's team. "Many companies have vision statements nicely framed and displayed on walls, but they don't live and breathe them. When I first heard about the three-legged stool, I thought it was just another slogan. But McDonald's is different. No one else shares a Plan to Win and asks us to align with their goals. I feel like I am part of McDonald's team, not just a supplier who sells them stuff until the next competitive bid cycle."[14]

Across the board, suppliers agree.

Carey Cooper, chief executive officer (CEO) of Danaco Solutions LLC, put the relationship in perspective. "It's not to say that McDonald's is all 'kumbaya.' They are incredibly demanding—but always fair. And they expect the same from us. Our employees fight to be on the McDonald's account. Who wouldn't want to work with a customer that treats you with such a high degree of respect and values your opinions?"[15]

GOVERNANCE STARTS WITH EXCELLING ON THE FUNDAMENTALS

Executives of a company the size of McDonald's could not sleep at night if they had issues with the basics, such as quality and safety. That is why McDonald's has established the toughest standards in the world for food handling and processing, known internally as QSC&V (Quality, Service, Cleanliness, and Value). For Jerome Lyman, vice president of McDonald's global supply chain, the company's commitment to quality and safety is serious business. He described his job as "keeping our CEO from testifying in a congressional review." His words may sound flippant, but the stakes are literally that high. "We have twelve nonnegotiables of safety, performance standards, and animal welfare. It's much easier to maintain our demanding standards when we know and trust our business partners intimately. The supplier has skin in the game, and we all share common goals. Anyone can fake an audit—and I find it comforting to know that our suppliers wouldn't even think of faking it." Lyman paused and shuddered when he considered the alternative. "I would not want to be in the shoes of a food company that has a multiplicity of suppliers. It must be an exhaustive effort."[16]

Lyman knows that suppliers themselves are just as bullish on quality and safety, embedding a rigorous and almost religious commitment to delivering safety and quality. This built-in maniacal culture around quality and safety lets Lyman sleep soundly at night because he knows suppliers take safety and quality just as seriously as he and his fellow quality team members. Suppliers such as Keystone Foods and Lopez Foods are proud—even boastful—of their ability to enable McDonald's to have the world's safest supply chain for food. Ed Sanchez, CEO of Lopez Foods, openly shares a video highlighting his company's hourly 100-point quality inspection process on McDonald's web site,[17] and Keystone opened its doors for a *USA Today* tour to show how its beef is "safer than a school kids' lunch." That is right. A 2009 article revealed that McDonald's tests its beef up to ten times more than companies selling beef to school programs.[18] (And beef sold to schools exceeds normal U.S. Department of Agriculture requirements for meat that is sold commercially through retail stores.)

The results? Restaurant goers around the world are comfortable knowing that a Big Mac is the same across the world as it is across town. Over 60 million visitors eat under the Golden Arches every day—uneventfully. Caroline Smith DeWaal, food safety director of the nonprofit Center for Science in the Public Interest in Washington, DC, confirms that McDonald's is "the top of the top."[19]

With food quality and safety covered, McDonald's can spend more time working with suppliers to create strategic value—such as increasing efficiencies, mitigating risk, and even creating new products. This effective collaboration starts with McDonald's commitment for building positive partnerships with suppliers.

GOVERNANCE: THE RELATIONSHIP MANAGEMENT STRUCTURE

The relationship management structure formulates and supports joint policies that emphasize the importance of building a collaborative working environment, attitudes, and behaviors. The structure is flexible, provides insights about meeting the desired outcomes, and strengthens the relationships between the parties.

To make relationships work properly, McDonald's uses several approaches that, when combined, create tight and transparent bonds between the company and its suppliers.

Peer-to-Peer Relationships

The term *peer to peer* (P2P) was coined to describe compatible technologies that communicate across equal platforms. Napster (which has now joined with Rhapsody) is an example of P2P networking. When we refer to peer-to-peer relationships within Vested relationships, we are talking about real people—individuals holding mirrored responsibilities within each partner company. These similarly tasked individuals form a partnership of their own and communicate continuously to solve problems and achieve goals.

McDonald's uses a P2P between suppliers and itself for each level—from operational to executive. The one-to-one alignment is a proactive approach to managing business. Ed Sanchez of Lopez Foods explained how it works. "The best part of McDonald's governance is the deep peer-to-peer relationships. Work takes place seamlessly on the peer-to-peer basis where problems are solved at the lowest level possible. If we have a problem, they get it. You don't have to educate McDonald's people on the problem—instead, our McDonald's counterparts are there to help us. But a key is they don't micromanage us."[20] Sanchez laughed and added, "For a different client, we were short one truck the other day, and the issue came all the way up to me. At McDonald's, it would never get to me. The right levels would just be on it and the problem would be fixed. I'd never hear about a short truck."

Sanchez paused and added a more personal dimension to the meaning of P2P relationships. "McDonald's wants the relationship with the person. If a person is assigned to the account, it is constant. To McDonald's, suppliers are part of the planning and execution of their Plan to Win. It's not just business—it's personal, and they want to see the person that is helping them succeed or fail." Sanchez knows that while day-to-day business is in the capable hands of the right people, it is important for him to have his own P2P connection with McDonald's senior management. This is done both formally and informally to help both parties ensure they stay in sync.

To manage the process and ensure a proper business rhythm, McDonald's initiates communication at multiple levels in multiple ways and uses various tools to provide 360-degree feedback in both formal and informal settings.

Monthly Metrics Report

Many primary suppliers receive monthly metrics reports comparing their performance to their counterparts in the System. The individual names and scores of competitors are not revealed; instead, the report presents a fact-based assessment of how the supplier ranks in its category compared to competitors. Sanchez related a time when Lopez Foods's monthly metrics spelled trouble. "We were in last position for a while with regard to costs and knew we had a problem. We started to see the warning signs as the metric trended downward, and it was a clear signal I needed to have personal involvement to correct the situation. We were having trouble getting to the bottom of why our costs were out of line. Our McDonald's counterparts jumped in and, together, we went line by line to break out costs and identify the underlying cause behind our costs issues. While we don't like these discussions, we know that McDonald's will help us turn the situation around and get back on track."

In this case, the issue turned out to be packaging problem. Sanchez added, "McDonald's and Lopez Foods put our heads together to find a solution. In no time we were back on track with our costs."

FORMAL QUARTERLY BUSINESS REVIEWS

Another regular interaction is the quarterly business review (QBR). At the beginning of the year, four dates are set aside for meetings. This allows parties to lock in the calendars of key people who need to be at the meetings. The group is relatively small, frequently about five people from the supplier and an equal number from McDonald's. The parties do go over key performance indicators, but the reviews go well beyond reviewing what happened in the past. The main focus of the QBR is strategic in nature. Time is spent on specific initiatives that are driving business improvements to help McDonald's achieve its Plan to Win goals. Reviews are used to proactively challenge the status quo, anticipate changes, and redefine mutual goals. QBRs also provide a structured way for McDonald's and its suppliers to talk about industry trends and market conditions and consider what needs to be done in the future.

Suppliers relate how important the QBRs are to the relationship and appreciate the formal nature of the QBR process. One supplier shared his perspective: "We live by QBRs. We want a very rigorous and formal QBR process because this is where we communicate our value and sync on performance against our value. At a minimum, we are connecting with key leaders quarterly. This is a basic component of a relationship, and, without this, I believe there is a slippery slope."

Site Visits

Yet another way McDonald's and suppliers strengthen their relationships is through up-close-and-personal on-site visits. Typically, about four times a year, a McDonald's representative travels to a supplier's facility to meet with the CEO and management team. For production suppliers, the joint team takes time to walk the floor of the factory, making certain QSC&V

standards are evident. The objective is to identify opportunities in the process that can positively impact the value chain. Together, McDonald's and suppliers discuss ways to solve problems blocking efficiencies, go through the financials, and look at the business going forward. It is important to point out that suppliers unanimously view these meetings as helpful; none interviewed perceived McDonald's to be micromanaging their business.

Ad Hoc and Social Gatherings

Suppliers working on specific business initiatives often participate in ad hoc meetings with their McDonald's counterparts and their competitors. For example, Mike Ward—a legendary baker at Fresh Start Bakeries—has traveled to over 25 countries to help solve baking issues and set up new suppliers.

Ward fondly recalled his favorite story about helping with the first McDonald's restaurant in Russia. Prior to the historic opening, the buns were found to be unsatisfactory. CEO Fred Turner was frustrated and personally called Ward to help get to the bottom of the problem. Ward's assessment? "It was very cold in Moscow, and the temperature was having a negative impact on the buns. The dough was not performing well in the chilly air." Ward and his team devised ways to warm the baking pans and raise the working temperature of the dough. "It took all night, but the next day we had real good buns."[21]

Ward recalled that the best part of his experience in Moscow was the grand opening itself. He stood in the lobby and stared down the street in amazement. "There was literally a sea of people, 40 wide and four miles long, waiting patiently to experience for themselves the magic of the Golden Arches. People had never eaten a burger before. I watched as people pulled them apart to examine them. When they were done, the customers saved everything—the wrappers, the packaging. It was amazing." Ward quietly admitted, "It's the only thing in business that ever brought me to tears."

McDonald's encourages suppliers to socialize outside of the office. This enables both parties to get to know the people behind the business, facilitating a better understanding of business needs. Ed Sanchez explained the McFamily culture: "It's not uncommon for McDonald's employees to ask about my daughter and how she's doing in school."[22] This culture dates back to Ray Kroc himself, who regularly invited his coworkers and suppliers to his house for dinner. Kroc—a former professional piano player in nightclubs—often played the piano and entertained.

Formal Supplier Events

Last, but not least, are the formal supplier gatherings, such as supplier summits and roundtables. The most formal of these meetings, the supplier summits, are held annually in the United States and every two years in other regions. All McDonald's suppliers are invited. With 400 to 600 people filling the room, suppliers hear from McDonald's top leaders, including senior management, as well as regional presidents and members of menu management. Francesca DeBiase explained, "The purpose is to give suppliers a really well-rounded understanding of where McDonald's is going. This meeting is extremely important."[23]

An essential aspect of the supplier summits is the awards dinner and presentations. Between 15 and 30 awards are presented, depending on the location. Award categories include "System First," "Sustainability," and "Innovation," to name a few. The crowning event is the coveted Supplier of the Year award. DeBiase continued, "It's a huge deal. The supplier who wins gets a visit from our entire senior management team—along with a festive party for the people who work on our account. These are really motivating."

In addition to supplier summits, McDonald's holds a global supplier roundtable, hosting one person from each of its top 15 or 16 strategic suppliers within a region. DeBiase explained the process: "We send them four or five open-ended questions ahead of time. Our goal is to really get an in-depth understanding of what we can do better. Are we living our values every day? Where should we be headed? What could we do better? Then we listen to their feedback." When themes develop, McDonald's integrates them into the Plan to Win. The process is important to McDonald's continuous improvement. DeBiase is passionate about the process. "We have done the roundtables for the last four years in order to ensure McDonald's continues to have the 'right' read from our global suppliers. Our suppliers keep us aligned, and we integrate their ideas. Roundtables truly are a critical component of helping us get better and keep the three-legged stool balanced."

McDonald's is not afraid to ask tough questions. For example, one of the questions was "Are we living the value of our supply chain principles at all levels and areas of the world?" The answer? Suppliers had confidence the highest levels of McDonald's management believed in and adhered to the guiding principles but perceived a behavior gap between the day-to-day people having to make tough decisions. DeBiase and her McDonald's colleagues took action. "In response, McDonald's held a supply chain symposium in 2011 that asked everyone around the world to focus on McDonald's Value of Supply Chain and close the gaps. We had several of our leaders provide real-world examples of what was going well and what was not going so well. Our goal was learning and improvement of McDonald's management consistency." DeBiase continued: "Another thing the United States did is create a sort of a council of elders for coaching newer team members when it comes to making key decisions about suppliers. This helps us sense-check we are living the values. We now consider this a best practice and are rolling it out in other regions around the world."

Managing the Meeting Maze

Customs and laws vary dramatically around the world. McDonald's supply chain team members meet with suppliers at regional/zone and country levels. McDonald's DeBiase admitted that keeping up with the various meetings can create a challenge in ensuring consistency of messaging across the world. "McDonald's consciously works to smooth the rough spots and strives for better consistency in their messaging with suppliers. And McDonald's expects suppliers to raise a red flag when they are getting mixed messages," she explained.

Although meetings do cost money in time and travel, McDonald's stands firm that the cost is worth it. DeBiase challenged outsiders who raise eyebrows at McDonald's extensive supplier relationship efforts. "How can you expect to manage the business effectively without having face-to-face meetings with your suppliers? For example, I take personal responsibility for meeting with each of our strategic suppliers on a quarterly basis to discuss our principles and behavior. It's one thing to achieve results, but we need to make sure we are all behaving in the right manner."

GOVERNANCE: TRANSFORMATION MANAGEMENT

McDonald's and its suppliers around the world are justifiably proud of the strong supply chain they have built. Just because McDonald's has the model nailed and can deliver reliably against stringent QSC&V standards, all three legs of the stool—corporate, owner/operators, and suppliers—need to constantly challenge each other to get better, bringing innovation to processes and products that enable McDonald's to lead competitors in terms of value for consumers.

Cargill's Pete Richter offered a supplier's viewpoint. "Cargill's institutional challenge is to understand that even though as a company, we are paid fairly when we perform—but we are required to continually reinvent ourselves. It doesn't matter if we have a one-year, three-year, or five-year handshake deal. We must *always* challenge the value add and innovate."[24]

McDonald's has learned that the potential for successful innovation is increased exponentially by strategies that institutionalize collaboration not only between McDonald's and the suppliers *but also between suppliers.*

In fact, McDonald's creates a virtual playground for suppliers to openly share breakthrough advancements with one another, feeding off each other to drive improvements that benefit not only McDonald's but the suppliers themselves. McDonald's consciously creates opportunities where it and suppliers engage in open dialog to solve some of the company's problems. Typically the venues are in the form of what is known as councils within the System. Although only a handful of the councils have authority to make decisions on behalf of McDonald's, all are taken seriously as a way to help the company openly debate ways to improve the System. Council meetings can be regionally or commodity focused, or formed by invitation. The forums provide venues for McDonald's to share plans, results, and market changes. Most important, suppliers share with one another new techniques and successes. The open communication strengthens the System as a whole and continuously improves quality standards.

The primary reason why suppliers are willing to share ideas and drive joint innovation ideas for McDonald's is the simple fact that, within the McDonald's System, everyone understands that they are trying to create wealth for all three legs of the stool. As they "grow the pie," there is more for all. McDonald's commitment to fairness and loyalty carves out a seat at the table for suppliers. Suppliers quickly grasp it is in their best interest to grow the pie versus fight over it with competitors. John Burke is executive vice president and CEO of Armada Supply Chain Solutions, a supply chain management and freight management services firm. Burke put in this way: "Suppliers have come to realize they really can't gain anything by not working with another supplier—but they can gain a lot if they can devise ways to improve overall System performance, such as reducing costs or increasing sales."[25]

People who are new to the System share their astonishment that McDonald's suppliers actually like working together. Eric Johnson, CEO of Baldwin-Richardson Foods, explained his reactions when he first came into the McDonald's System in 1997. "Outside of McDonald's, most of the suppliers are typically in a short-term, win-lose environment that is typically cutthroat, trying to win the next big RFP [request for proposal] or purchase order. At McDonald's, I found myself sitting at the same table and engaging in discussions about how we could all partner to make real impacts for the System. No other customer I had ever dealt with was even close to this kind of collaboration." Johnson continued, "At McDonald's I quickly learned that it is much better (and fun) to grow the pie than worry about how big your slice is today. There is plenty for all."[26]

Product Advisory Councils

A key part of McDonald's governance is the use of product councils that are comprised of suppliers of the category or commodity, plus representatives from the owner/operators' association and McDonald's Corporation. The product councils are working groups, committed to the advancement of the System and achievement of the Plan to Win. The objective is to establish an open, debating culture that addresses important issues and ultimately writes business models and strategies for a certain commodity. During the meetings, suppliers share approaches and brainstorm better ways to manage supply within the category.

Gary Johnson explains the value of the Global Poultry Supplier Advisory Council, which represents a majority of McDonald's worldwide poultry resources. "The council helps identify key supply chain trends that impact poultry supply. They also weigh in where McDonald's should focus energy to ensure the best poultry supply chain strategy." Johnson is proud of the council's work, and McDonald's has incorporated many of its suggestions into its global poultry strategy.

Each of the major commodity areas has a council that includes beef, poultry, bakery, dairy, and produce. It is a working group, committed to the advancement of the System and achieving the Plan to Win. Pete Richter, chair of the U.S. Supplier Advisory Council, relates, "Product councils give suppliers a chance to be heard with regard to how the System should manage a commodity. Suppliers share approaches and brainstorm better ways to manage supply and mitigate risks within the category. More importantly, the councils are a critical part of McDonald's culture—the willingness to listen. It's not 15 people showing up for lunch. McDonald's is very interested in learning and takes the recommendations from the product councils very seriously."

Richter clarifies the councils' benefit: "If the suppliers are fragmented—you don't drive change. The product councils give suppliers an opportunity work in harmony and come to agreement on matters that matter to the System." Typical discussions in a product council are how do we get a higher percentage of raw materials on a fixed price contract? Or, how do we mitigate risk? Richter explains the importance of this to the McDonald's System. "The product councils give suppliers a venue for working together where they are not competing. When suppliers work in harmony they almost always have ideas that build on top of each other—driving a higher degree of innovation for McDonald's."

Contingency planning is a perfect example of the role product councils play. Suppliers collaborate to create comprehensive, specific blueprints to meet any emergency condition that could develop, whether it is a quality or safety issue or loss of assured supply due to disaster. OSI Group's[27] vice president, McDonald's North American business team leader Michael

Boccio, explained the value of working closely with his competitors: "There was a time when a competitor built a new facility in southern China. To their surprise, it turned out the Chinese military had an old munitions dump located directly under the neighborhood where the building was located. The supplier only became aware of this fact after a huge explosion happened underneath their plant one afternoon while the plant was closed. It took out about 20 square blocks and sent a cloud plume two and a half miles into the sky that required diversion of air traffic at nearby Hong Kong International Airport. The contingency plan was in place. The OSI Group immediately trucked product the 1,500 miles to ensure McDonald's restaurants had assured supply and quality until the other supplier was able to recover. When things happen...all we have to do is pick up the phone."[28]

When there is a contingency situation, the supply community circles the wagons to make sure McDonald's supply to the restaurants is not in jeopardy. Jose-Luis Bretones-Lopez, Director of Worldwide Supply Chain Strategy, works with McDonald's strategic sourcing and credits suppliers with amazing success stories. "Because of our suppliers, we find the supplies we need. For example—the floods in Australia and how horrible they were. We were able to get supplies to the restaurants against all odds. It's a very typical thing that everyone is scrambling. Distribution centers are completely ruined. Roads are impassable. Grasslands are flooded. But because of that strong commitment, we get food to restaurants."[29]

Food Improvement Team

The food improvement teams in each area of the world have been granted authority to make decisions regarding changes in one of McDonald's most protected priorities—the menu. Owner/operators, suppliers, and McDonald's run this group, studying options and passing final judgment on what is on—or off—the menu. Naturally, any new menu items are approved through the food improvement team, but, more important, ways to improve and meet the public's changing needs and tastes are ongoing topics for consideration. McDonald's core menu cannot be changed without the team's approval.

An example of a recent improvement approved by the U.S. food improvement team is the invention of a new cooking device for beef patties that reduces cooking time. The new device allows the patties to be removed from the grill at the same time, ensuring taste consistency as well as a cleaner grill surface. The food improvement team approved the new cooking device after McDonald's research kitchens perfected the exact optimum cooking time and temperature for patties.

Most people might think a second or two of cooking time would not a make a difference. But, to McDonald's, details matter. And whether it is equipment, ingredients, calorie count, or bread texture, the food improvement teams make certain QSC&V are maintained.

Joint Development Initiatives

Vested relationships almost always look to suppliers for innovation. However, it is rare that companies ask suppliers—competitors, if you will—to work with one another to find ways to innovate. That is exactly what happened with BAMA, a supplier of apple pies. CEO Mark Bendix moved to BAMA from a Fortune 500 company and was unaccustomed to McDonald's transparent and collaborative ways. He related this story: "Early on in my tenure, about 2006, McDonald's asked us to work on a project with one of our primary competitors. I had never worked on a project or product together with a competitor. In other food service companies where institutional knowledge is developed, you talk about partnership, but it's rarely real. But we did it. Working collaboratively from conception, to thought process, to origination, to test, to market. True sharing. The light went on for me. While different, this was a truly better way."[30] The experience helped Bendix get ketchup in his veins, a term used in the McDonald's System for when a person has become fully committed to System First thinking. The real proof actually came after the fact for Bendix. "We got so much value out of working with our competitor, we continue to work cooperatively on business together. Simply put, I quickly learned to System First thinking works."

Another example of joint development initiatives is how McDonald's works with nongovernmental organizations (NGOs) and suppliers on sustainability. Gary Johnson, senior director of the worldwide supply chain, led a sustainability strategy for how McDonald's procures fish for the Filet-O-Fish sandwich. The program brought together McDonald's, its Filet-O-Fish suppliers, and the NGO Conservation International with the goal to develop a sustainable supply chain strategy. "The suppliers were concerned about having an NGO on the team because we had never done that before. But they trusted me that it would work, and it did. We developed the Sustainable Fish Standards, which are still in place today."[31]

Supplier Advisory Councils

McDonald's expectation that suppliers will collaborate with each other for the overall benefit of the System is formalized within the regional Supplier Advisory Councils. In the United States the council is comprised of about 20 suppliers, handpicked by McDonald's management team. These men and women meet three times a year to fulfill a mission of supplier representation and dialog. McDonald's senior management listens carefully to the council discussions; top McDonald's leaders always are present during the meetings.

There is also extreme transparency about future plans and present problems. McDonald's opens its world to the Supplier Advisory Councils, sharing details regarding what is going on within the company and asking for feedback.

John Burke of Armada Supply Chain Solutions gave his perspective: "Conversations go beyond supply chain and procurement. We get remarkable insight from people elsewhere in the organization. And we offer feedback to McDonald's about issues with which they wrestle. For example, 'How should we structure our Rewards for Excellence program? Or, 'What's the best way to approach suppliers?' "[32]

GOVERNANCE: EXIT MANAGEMENT

One might think that a handshake deal is open-ended permission for McDonald's to switch suppliers—or for a supplier to take advantage of McDonald's. But the social contract that binds McDonald's and its suppliers is stronger than the written word. When McDonald's and a supplier part ways, it is called an "exit," and it is a big deal. Simply put, the consequences for a supplier are huge, and the costs of switching for McDonald's are high. For these reasons, McDonald's and its suppliers continuously strive for System First thinking, behavior that keeps both parties tightly aligned.

"Thankfully, supplier exits are very rare," asserted Dan Gorsky, senior vice president of McDonald's North America Supply Chain. "In my tenure of 18 years at McDonald's, I can count the number of supplier exits on one hand. In the very rare case, a supplier does violate the inviolable quality, food safety, and animal welfare standards, such as a supplier that did not meet our animal welfare standards for chicken handling and did not instill confidence in us that they would be able to consistently over time."[33] The consequence? Immediate exit for that supplier.

But suppliers are not always perfect on everything. For example, some slip on cost competitiveness, and others struggle to drive innovation for McDonald's—both sources of the chain's competitive advantage. Gorsky continued: "Typically, when a supplier struggles, for a period of time—numerous conversations and contingency plans ensue. Ultimately, a supplier can be put on probation." If the supplier cannot reach the required standards, McDonald's will stop doing business with it. But it's a rare occasion. The initial vetting process and the support offered by McDonald's and other suppliers usually make the situation work.

Although suppliers rarely exit the System, McDonald's does complete a "category realignment" every two to three years based on the category. Realignment can happen for a variety of reasons, but the goal of realignment is to balance McDonald's portfolio of requirements across its supply base in a fair and equitable manner.

In some cases, McDonald's realigns a category based on a supplier's performance, shifting market share from suppliers that are not meeting their mutually agreed-upon Plan to Win goals and basic key performance indicators.

Devin Cole, group vice president of the Food Service Division of Tyson Foods, shared how McDonald's approaches realignment. "Trust is the basic building block of McDonald's supplier relationships and is a fragile thing which can be eroded through the actions of a single individual if not relentlessly protected. Tyson has been a longtime supplier of McDonald's, but new leadership in our company managed—or, more appropriately, mismanaged—the McDonald's account. Tyson started to treat McDonald's like every other customer, and the magic dissipated as the fundamentals of trust and collaboration were lost with Tyson's management turnover. Tyson got complacent as a supplier and our performance slipped."[34]

When Cole was tapped for the lead role in managing the McDonald's account, Tyson Foods was not a favored supplier. Cole remembered: "It was us that had gotten off track. McDonald's consistently adhered to their values and rewards. They held themselves accountable and remained open to talking with us, even when we weren't holding up our end. McDonald's always had a willingness to meet with me and coach me on how Tyson could get back on a path to mutual success."

Cole was determined to regain McDonald's trust and worked hard to return to the culture of mutual trust and respect that Ray Kroc put in place over 30 years ago. When McDonald's asked Cole to mentor, support, and help a new supplier that took over a portion of the business Tyson had lost, Cole knew it was the right thing to do. "Our team had trepidation about the assignment. After all, this was business over which Tyson once had control and lost due to poor performance." But Cole was adamant. "We are responsible for losing this business. Now we're going to be responsible to make sure McDonald's has the assured supply it needs...even when that means helping our competition."

Tyson reluctantly sent a team to the new supplier's factory to assist. As it turns out, Tyson's reluctance was insignificant compared to the new supplier's fear. The Tyson team members were not allowed onto the factory floor at the competitor business but were forced to spend the entire day in a waiting room, unable to observe operations and make recommendations. Cole reported back to McDonald's: "We can't help them unless you can help us get in the door." Eventually, McDonald's convinced the new supplier to accept assistance from Tyson. But in the end this supplier could not live within the McDonald's System First approach and was exited from the McFamily.

Cole rebuilt the partnership trust and tries to maintain the unique relationship within the Tyson corporate environment. "Not everyone understands how the McDonald's relationship works. The rest of the world I live in often thinks we act foolishly—that working without contracts can cause the company to get burned. Working with McDonald's requires a leap of faith. But it's a leap worth taking because, time and time again, McDonald's proves themselves to be true partners that reward you with increased business and opportunities." Cole is aware of the power of a trusting handshake and zealously oversees the Tyson team to protect the values for long-term relationship success. "We make sure all our team thinks about is McDonald's. It's a culture we guard because we have seen what can happen. Typically, somebody blinks and screws it up. If you don't have the right people advocating for McDonald's, it can quickly go south. My job is to keep Tyson true to System First thinking, which ultimately leads to Tyson being rewarded in the long term."

And reward is sweet, indeed. Tyson won back more business and eventually was named McDonald's 2010 Supplier of the Year. For Cole, winning became real when he visited Don Tyson, president and CEO of Tyson Foods from 1967 to 1991. Cole personally told him that the company had reestablished itself in the same tradition that started between Don and Ray Kroc. Although it might not be easy, large public companies can understand the importance of the long-term, System First approach.

Tyson's comeback is a win for McDonald's as well. Dan Gorsky expressed McDonald's pride and commitment to continuous improvement at the U.S. supplier summit in September 2011. "We truly love it when suppliers bounce back from their down performance periods. In every instance that I can think of, the supplier has come back a stronger, more robust, more focused, more competitive and innovative business partner. It is one of the most fulfilling parts of what we do together when this happens."[35]

Poor performance is one reason for a category realignment, but there are other reasons. One is changing market conditions. As consumer tastes evolve, sometimes McDonald's realigns a supplier's market share based on volumes of a certain commodity decreasing. One example is Lopez Foods, a beef supplier, which was recently awarded the opportunity to expand into the poultry category as consumer demand for chicken increased. In other cases, new menu offerings—such as coffee, salads, and smoothies—explode onto the market, and the only way McDonald's can have assured supply is to add new suppliers. For example, when McDonald's added fruit smoothies to its menu, it had to add new suppliers as well as work with established partners.

Often, during a realignment, suppliers with the best performance are awarded additional business. Many times they are offered an opportunity to establish new lines of business, as with Lopez Foods, or they are asked if they are interested in expanding into new regions. One good example comes from Chip Klosterman of Klosterman Bakeries. Chip wanted to expand his bakery business internationally and was pleased when McDonald's offered him an opportunity to provide baked goods in the new market of Puerto Rico. McDonald's had been working with local suppliers there after entering the market but was unhappy with the quality it was receiving. McDonald's and Klosterman agreed that it made sense for Klosterman to make a capital investment to build a new facility in Puerto Rico. In classic MacDonald's style, a simple handshake sealed the deal, and Klosterman invested heavily in the Puerto Rico operations.

As time went by, the volume Klosterman needed to make the dedicated Puerto Rico bakery profitable did not materialize. But without a contract, Klosterman did not have a way to alleviate risk for his company. So he did what all suppliers do when things do not work out as planned after a handshake deal with McDonald's. He went back to McDonald's, and the two companies sat shoulder to shoulder to figure out what could be done. The parties identified three options: (1) sell the bakery, (2) close the bakery, or (3) add third-party competitor products into the mix.

McDonald's selfishly could have stuck Klosterman with the loss. But that is win-lose thinking and would have violated a core tenet of ensuring that all three legs of the stool remain strong. The decision was made to allow Klosterman to sell bakery products to McDonald's competitors in order for him to cover his costs. Of course, McDonald's would have preferred Klosterman to refrain from offering better quality to competing restaurants, but it came down to this question: What is in the best interest of the System? System First thinking wants suppliers to be profitable.

Klosterman reflected on the situation. "It was pretty easy to capture new business through the bakery since we had a clear competitive advantage with quality and efficiency over other local bakeries. Once the volume was up, it became easy to sell the bakery, and that is what we did."[36] But the story does not end there.

Unfortunately, the new supplier did not fully understand the McDonald's expectations, and another change was needed. To ensure quality and steady supply, McDonald's eventually decided to move to a mixed model, relying on a combination of baked goods from local suppliers *and* from trusted North America suppliers. McDonald's reassigned some of the work to Tennessee Bun—a joint venture Klosterman had built years before with Fresh Start Bakeries and business partner Cordia Harrington.

Klosterman observed, "My take is that, as a McDonald's supplier, we are not married to a specific model; we are married to some basic operating principles of fairness, competitiveness, and continuous improvement. It turns out that the mixed supply model has been beneficial for all."

He offered advice about working with McDonald's. "You cannot dictate the three-legged stool approach to a supplier. The supplier has to understand it and believe in it. The trust is so deep it's almost a faith that you know you will just be treated fairly. If a supplier does not get it, then McDonald's has to look at the supplier differently. In the end the suppliers need to be aligned to last. Without alignment, neither party can get into the spirit to develop trust."

WHO'S MINDING THE THREE-LEGGED STOOL?

A decided advantage for McDonald's is the positive power of its self-governance culture. System First thinking challenges both McDonald's and suppliers to do the right thing when it comes to the business. The partnership is a two-way street. McDonald's challenges suppliers to deliver on QSC&V and continuously innovate, and suppliers challenge McDonald's to make smart supply chain decisions. "It is easier to make a supply chain decision that can suboptimize the System. But when you have restaurant owners/operators and suppliers challenging your decision constantly, it keeps you on your toes and ensures the best value for our customers," explained Gary Johnson, senior director of the worldwide supply chain. "It's not just buying products—it really is about managing the *business*."[37]

McDonald's suppliers take the partnership concept seriously. Expectations rise to levels normally reserved for a company's employees. Ted Perlman, chairman of HAVI Global Solutions, remembered an occasion when he found himself in hot water with McDonald's.[38] HAVI performs packaging services, promotions management and analytics, and supply chain services for McDonald's. Perlman implemented a McDonald's *corporate* decision to use a thinner, cheaper paper for the french fry bag. The flimsier bag proved too pliable for stores, and crews put too few or too many fries in them. It was a mess. When Fred Turner—CEO of McDonald's at the time—learned of the mistake, he was not only angry with the McDonald's manager who ordered the change, he was also angry with Perlman. Turner expressed displeasure that Perlman had *allowed* the McDonald's manager to mess around with McDonald's most important product. Perlman thinks about the lesson learned frequently and admitted, "My whole role in life as a supplier is not letting McDonald's consciously make a mistake."

Perlman joined the ranks of McDonald's partners who retain their supplier status by keeping the question What's best for the System? their top focus. In Perlman's case, that meant understanding that his job was not simply to fulfill requests of McDonald's managers but also to question decisions that could negatively impact the brand.

Vigilance for values ensures that the historic win-win-win strategic alliances among employees, restaurant owner/operators, and suppliers will continue in the future. And McDonald's stands shoulder to shoulder with suppliers to help make the System the best it can possibly be.

VESTED FOR SUCCESS

Many have credited McDonald's with transforming the food industry. John Love, an authority on the company, wrote about its influence on the industry:

> McDonald's greatest impact on American business is in areas that consumers do not see. In their search for improvements, McDonald's operations specialists moved back down the food and equipment supply chain. They changed the way farmers grow potatoes and the way companies process them. They introduced new methods to the nation's dairies. They altered the way ranchers raised beef and the way the meat industry makes the final product. They invented the most efficient cooking equipment the food service industry had seen. They pioneered new methods of food packaging and distribution. Indeed, no one has had more impact than McDonald's in modernizing food processing and distribution in the past four decades.[39]

But ask anyone at McDonald's, and he or she will tell you the company could not have done it alone. Success came with the entrepreneurship and leadership of McDonald's suppliers. And one of the primary reasons suppliers invested in innovations on McDonald's behalf was Ray Kroc's long-term and fair approach to dealing with them. Suppliers learned they could develop deep relationships with McDonald's based on levels of trust they had never experienced with other companies.

Suppliers, a key leg in the three-legged stool, know that they do not just have a seat at the table; they are a critical part of making the System work. The more successful the System, the more successful all the players in the System become. Indeed, the success of McDonald's employees, restaurant owner/operators, and suppliers speaks for itself.

When you look back at McDonald's success, the results are simply staggering. But probably one of the best testaments to McDonald's values and long-term thinking is the fact that in the midst of short-term pressures of a global recession, the company nevertheless has experienced exceptional performance.[40] McDonald's proudly shares results in its annual reports. Global comparable sales achieved their ninth consecutive year of same-store sales growth. In 2011, McDonald's topped the Dow Jones charts, leading all 30 of the components of the Dow Jones Industrial Average.[41]

But excellence goes well beyond financial success. In 2011, *Fortune* magazine named McDonald's the #10 Most Admired Company in the World. It also ranked McDonald's #1 among all companies for Management Quality for "Global Competitiveness, and Use of Corporate Assets," and #2 among all companies for "Best Long-Term Investment." *Barron's* ranked the company #5 on its 2011 list of Most Respected Companies. *Businessweek* included it in its top 20 Best Companies for Leadership and wrote that McDonald's was one of the greenest companies in the world. McDonald's has earned dozens more awards and deserved recognition in vital areas of workplace, diversity, and sustainability.

McDonald's executives get top honors as well. *Chief Executive Magazine* named recently retired Jim Skinner CEO of the Year in 2009, and *Businessweek* called him one of 2010's 10 Most Innovative

People. But it is McDonald's unequivocal commitment to the business system of the three-legged stool that elevates it to #1 every day. All three legs of the stool work for the benefit of each other as well as themselves because when everyone is successful, there is greater reward for all.

Together, McDonald's, its owner/operators, and its suppliers have created a System to be reckoned with—a System that continues to set records after 50 years.

7

ONE SIZE FITS ALL: HOW THE VESTED FIVE RULES BRING TRANSFORMATION TO ORGANIZATIONS OF ALL TYPES AND SIZES

The case studies we have shared so far have focused on very large organizations that made a choice to use Vested principles from the start of their business relationships. When Procter & Gamble and Microsoft decided to outsource, they made the choice to build Vested relationships from the beginning. The Minnesota Department of Transportation (MnDOT) and the Department of Energy researched options and took the road less traveled when they deployed a Vested approach. Ray Kroc made a conscious decision to establish Vested thinking with his suppliers when he founded McDonald's over 50 years ago.

But can Vested work for smaller businesses or nonprofits? What about all those companies that have existing relationships? Can they "convert" to the Vested approach?

The answer is yes, yes, and yes. We have seen Vested principles applied in small businesses, nonprofits, and existing relationships with a great deal of success. Simply put: The principles work no matter what industry you are in or how large your organization is. This chapter provides highlights from our favorite examples of Vested by nonprofit and small businesses. We also profile a company that decided to convert an existing relationship to a Vested relationship.

WATER FOR PEOPLE

Ned Breslin began his career with Water For People in 2006 and became chief executive officer (CEO) in 2008; his passion for the cause is evident. His years of living in Africa and seeing the misery up close and personal often make his quiet voice sound deeply sad. Breslin was a country representative in Mozambique at WaterAid, an international nongovernmental organization (NGO) dedicated to the provision of safe domestic water, sanitation, and hygiene education to the world's poorest people. Ned lived there for more than a decade with his wife and young daughters and witnessed women and children walking miles every day just to get enough water to drink and cook.

Water For People is not just a vision; it is a 501(c)(3) nonprofit organization based in Denver, Colorado. It was founded in February 1991 by three dedicated individuals: Ken Miller, an executive with CH2M HILL and former president of the American Water Works Association (AWWA), the authoritative resource on safe water in North America and beyond; Wayne Weiss, vice president of Black & Veatch International, an infrastructure development firm; and John B. Mannion, a former executive director of AWWA. All three men believed that clean water is a basic human right.

Water For People's raison d'être is clear and not simply a nice slogan on its web site but rather something lived passionately in the Denver headquarters and the countries in which it operates.

> Water For People works to build a world where all people have access to safe drinking water and sanitation, and where no one suffers or dies from a water- or sanitation-related disease. This is our vision.
>
> We're on a mission. We work with people and partners to develop innovative and long-lasting solutions to the water, sanitation, and hygiene problems in the developing world. We strive to continually improve, to experiment with promising new ideas, and to leverage resources to multiply our impact.

What is different about Water For People is not its passion. Clearly, passion inspires action in all nonprofit organizations. Without it, NGOs would not exist. However, passion without discipline creates activity but not necessarily progress. And certainly not excellence. What sets Water For People apart is its approach—its *Vested* approach—to following the Vested Five Rules for working with partners to help to make their vision a reality.

The focus on long-term sustainable solutions means Water For People has to start with alliances that are long term and sustainable themselves. Simply put, this NGO relies on highly Vested commitments from the local communities it enters. Sometimes it applies rules differently from how for-profit organizations might, but rules are clearly present.

RULE #1: FOCUS ON OUTCOMES, NOT TRANSACTIONS

Ned Breslin believes one of the keys to Water For People's success is changing the way success is measured. The traditional way to measure success for water poverty is counting how many people gain access to water. Breslin passionately believes true success comes not just from getting people access to water but by building competent communities that can *sustain* their water supply.

This belief system stems from Breslin's firsthand observations of past approaches. The countrysides of many developing countries are littered with broken wells and pumps. Women and children walk by remnants of good intentions and wasted money as they trudge to rivers to retrieve unclean water. The equipment works for a few months, but once it breaks down, citizens don't have skills to repair it. The equipment is useless and merely serves to build distrust for the next NGO that comes around. It is estimated an average of 30 percent of installed water points are broken down; in some areas, such as the Democratic Republic of Congo, it's 60 percent.

If money were the answer, this problem would already be solved.[1] Harold Lockwood of AguaConsult, reported, "Twenty years ago, we identified one billion people without access to water. Since then, we have poured billions of dollars into the problem (an average of $3.4 billion annually) and we still have about the same number of people without water. We're doing something wrong."[2]

Some NGOs simply install water systems as gifts and assume that beneficiaries will have water for the foreseeable future. Obviously, that paradigm does not work. A more durable solution is required. And Water For People thinks it has a solution.

One of the keys to Water For People's success is its strategic long-term Vested partnerships with local governments and communities, partnerships that maximize the partners' ability to solve their own water poverty challenges through creative water and sanitation investments. Breslin explained, "What sustainability means to us is that beneficiaries counted today can still get safe water from functioning taps or pumps in ten years.

And when it's time for a new water system, beneficiaries and local government partners can replace the hardware themselves without seeking financial and technical help from yet another development organization. Sustainability means that people who start using a latrine today will never have to go to the bathroom outside again. And when the pit fills up, they can sell the contents for compost, or call a pit-emptying service, or replace their pit latrine."[3]

Keeping laser-like focus on the outcome reinforces Water For People's determination to achieve and at the same time allows for flexibility in *how* each local government and community solves its water poverty problem.

RULE #2: FOCUS ON THE *WHAT*, NOT THE *HOW*

When it comes to the details of how best to deploy and maintain water systems, Water For People looks to local communities for the best answers. No one size fits all. One example of the NGO's efforts is in the Bengali region in India, where Dipak Huziet and his fellow bike-riding mechanics are known as the Jalabandhu. *Jalabandhu* literally means "friends of water."[4] The Jalabandhu are part of a private-sector program launched by Water For People and local partners Sunderban Social Development Center and Sabuj Sangha in West Bengal. Water For People provides each mobile mechanic with training, a bicycle, and the tools necessary to repair and maintain the district's water infrastructure. In the beginning, the local government, with financial support from Water For People, paid the Jalabandhu. As the program matures, the mechanics become self-sufficient, private entrepreneurs who earn their wages directly from the communities they serve. It is all part of the cycle of sustainability: At first, both local villages and the Jalabandhu need assistance. In time, communities develop their own fee structures and accountable governance to maintain their own water supplies.

Beginning with only 8 water points under his supervision, Huziet grew his customer base to more than 77 water points. His excellent service is winning him new business. For example, in 2009, when Cyclone Aila hit, Huziet and other Jalabandhu worked tirelessly to repair 295 water points in just days. Villagers witnessed their efforts, were impressed, and signed on to the service. The mobile mechanics are on their way to self-sufficiency as more villages hire them to maintain water points. Building up local businesses is one of Water For People's creative strategies to increase the life span and decrease downtime of each water point and to create long-lasting water sanitation solutions.

In another example, Water For People is working within the area of Chinda in northern Honduras. About 5,000 people live within the 43-square-mile territorial extension, making a living through subsistence agriculture, livestock, and crafts.

Just as schools provide a natural activity center for small towns in the United States, so it is also in developing countries. Governing organizations such as parent-teacher associations (PTAs) and education boards provide a source of already-established leadership that can be tapped for constructing water and sanitation projects.

In Chinda, Water For People worked with the schools and PTAs to create the School Water, Sanitation and Hygiene Plus (SWASH+) community impact program. The program grants significant authority to the PTA of each community school.

After Water For People completes assessments and testing, it identifies a menu of options that could provide a stable, safe water service. The NGO then empowers the local governing bodies (frequently the PTAs) to select the technology infrastructure and manage the funds entrusted to them by governments and Water For People for construction. This includes keeping minutes of meetings, receipts, documentation of progress, and inventory control.

In Chinda, the agreement stipulates the PTA president supervises the contractor. But supervision in this case is extremely hands-on. President Marvin Fajardo joined other PTA members pounding picks into the earth, digging trenches for the pipes to be laid. Fajardo explained, "People say I come here because they pay me. But, no, we don't get paid at all." But for Fajardo, the work is a small price to pay for clean water for his children.

Once the system is in place, teachers instruct residents in both toilet and hand-washing habits. Volunteers are trained to make house calls to ensure that householders follow basic health safety at home as well as at school.

RULE #3: CLEARLY DEFINED AND MEASURABLE DESIRED OUTCOMES

Water For People believes that the chances for success increase when those involved have a commitment to work toward a limited number of strategic, long-term results. The fact that the NGO measures the efficacy of results at three, six, and ten years from each project's inception date is of particular significance. By measuring results over the long term, Water For People ensures that old programs are still up and running, new programs are built to last, and promises are kept. For this reason, the NGO invests time up front to collaborate with local partners and establish explicit definitions about how success is measured. Each and every project agreement defines what needs to be accomplished as well as what success will look like.

For example, a memorandum for the Rulindo Challenge includes an entire section called "Measures of Success." The memorandum states:

The Rulindo Challenge will be successful if:

5.1   All villages and public institutions of the Rulindo District have water supplies from the Government of Rwanda by the end of 2014. Water systems will, as best as possible, achieve government standards with respect to access (within 500 meters), for quantity (20 liters per person per day), and water quality (according to MININFRA [Government of Rwanda, Ministry of Infrastructure] guidelines for water quality).

5.2 Downtime of water facilities averages less than one day.

5.3 A monitoring program is in place that demonstrates project functionality and sustainability.

5.4 A funding mechanism is implemented that covers the costs of system repairs and replacements in the future so that no additional external finance is required.

5.5 Water system extensions occur to keep pace with population growth.

5.6 A similar initiative is started in at least one other district without financial support from Water For People.[5]

To measure actual success, Water For People turns to technology to help ensure that the water is still running. In 2008, the NGO launched a platform that it developed with Gallatin Systems called FLOW: Field Level Operations Watch, which broadcasts reports about the operational status of water projects around the world. FLOW utilizes Android cell phones to collect data. Using surveys, pictures, and videos on devices equipped with Global Positioning Systems, staff and volunteers upload real-time or close to real-time (depending on connectivity) information to Google Earth maps and Internet-based databases. Dashboards and maps help Water For People's program staff to quickly identify trends and problems. Peer organizations, governments, and donors can also see the information online. Taking a virtual journey to witness a project in action is as easy as pointing and clicking. The web site injects a whole new level of transparency, efficiency, and accountability into the work of Water For People as well as that of multiple other organizations that employ the technology.[6]

For practical purposes, the only thing required to keep FLOW up to date is a Wi-Fi connection—something every Water For

People country office has. The data that are captured are invaluable, providing inspiration and guidance for ongoing efforts.

RULE #4: PRICING MODEL WITH INCENTIVES

In a nonprofit organization, donations flow in and investments flow out. What makes Water For People different from many nonprofits is that it ultimately wants to work itself out of business by having local communities manage and maintain safe water supplies.

One strategy the NGO uses is to ensure that local communities are intimately involved from beginning to perpetuity of any endeavor, which ensures accountability for long-term success. Shared investment becomes an important focus. When leaders of Cuchumuela, Bolivia, offered a handkerchief holding $1,000 to Water For People to help pay for new water projects, they committed to help make the projects a success. When the people of Cuchemuela committed, Water For People committed.

"At first, the municipal sanitation unit had no equipment or facilities, and I was the only staff person," said Elvis Rivero Robles, Cuchumuela's director of basic sanitation. "Partnerships and shared investment became a very important strategy for us, and, through this, Cuchumuela is intent on protecting its hard work to build and maintain its water and sanitation systems."

Water For People invests its resources with local entrepreneurs, civil society, governments, and communities that commit their own energies and resources to ensure long-term, infectious results. They form Vested partnerships.

Water For People also ensures sustainability by working with its partners to set up municipalities or community water boards that set appropriate household fees (tariffs) to cover costs of water system maintenance and repair.

The fiscal component changes from project to project, agreement to agreement, depending on circumstances. If a household is headed by a child or infirm elderly person, the water board may subsidize or waive the water fee. The Rulindo Challenge, for instance, divides financial contributions among the partners by a percentage of total project cost. The government of Rwanda and the district commit to providing a minimum of 30 percent of the costs of the technology investment. Local communities must contribute 15 percent, and Water For People makes up the difference. A most important factor, however, is the clear provision that there will be a next project executed without the financial support of Water For People. This is done to ensure that independent sustainability remains viable and to build working models that can be replicated.

RULE #5: INSIGHT VERSUS OVERSIGHT GOVERNANCE

A key difference in Water For People's governance and the previous cases we have profiled is that the organization constructs literally hundreds of Vested agreements with multiple governments, NGOs and individuals. Each agreement contains shared risks, investments, and commitments with the ultimate goal of independence and sustainability.

Although individual agreements vary widely, the ethics that drive each and every commitment are constant. The Water For People website lists "Four Guiding Principles—One Human Need." The principles form the consistent policy that underpins all action.

- **We believe in people:** We respect the dignity of all people.
- **We keep it local:** We believe that water, sanitation, and hygiene problems are most effectively solved using local resources.
- **We keep good company:** We search out trusted partners who share our vision and work together to build long-term relationships based on trust.

- **We keep our promises:** We believe we owe it to the communities we serve, our volunteers, staff, and donors to act with integrity and manage our resources effectively and efficiently.[7]

The four principles comprise consistent strategies within Water For People's overall purpose: to work within defined regions to achieve 100 percent sustainable access to safe water. Although tools and technologies change, case by case, Water For People always adheres to these principles.

To manage operations in each country, Water For People establishes offices that are run and staffed mostly by native employees who know the politics, culture, language, and communities served. Currently, Water For People is active in 11 countries: Malawi, Rwanda, and Uganda in Africa; the state of West Bengal in India; Guatemala, Honduras, Nicaragua, and the Dominican Republic in Central America; and Bolivia, Ecuador, and Peru in South America. Its goal is for others—governments and development organizations—to replicate its model in new regions.

Prior to setting up a country office, Water For People registers with a country's national government. As it wants to be in countries for the long term, the NGO makes certain the proper authorities sanction efforts within each area. Registration ensures compatibility with local regulations. In CEO Breslin's opinion, this registration process is a matter of respect. "If a group came into my neighborhood in Denver and started to drill bore holes and lay pipes to deliver water in a new way, they'd be arrested," he explained.

Underpinning each commitment is the support and guidance of the Water For People organization. A favorite saying of Breslin is "broad and deep" because he wants leadership to come from the field and to be comprehensive and well researched. At the time this book went to press, there were 48 global-level staff members in Denver. It is in the country offices, however, where the vision turns into reality. In-country directors lead those offices, which are staffed by 10 to 20 workers per office.

The next step is working with local groups to identify regions in which to start work. Decisions are based on need and potential for enduring partnerships. Chinda is a good example. Water For People's country director for Honduras traveled there to meet with the mayor, who agreed to create a municipal water and sanitation office. Together, they went to Chinda communities, eventually signed three-party (Water For People, regional government, and local governing body) cooperation agreements, and began operations by constructing the water and sanitation infrastructure in each locality.[8]

As each household gains access to water service, personal contracts are executed with the community water board. The individual household contracts specify use and care of systems as well as any financial obligation that may apply. Water For People, once again, provides capacity-building training for committee volunteers. In Chinda, the water board treasurer, Mariano de Jesus Castejon, said: "Water For People taught us how to approach people and help monitor use of systems. We ask users to sign contracts so they commit to pay their fees and on time."

Chinda's story presents some of the variety of Vested partnerships necessary to overcome difficult challenges. Although authority is shared, governance duties are clearly defined. Other geographic regions may use alternate choices of partners, technologies, and processes, but generally all agreements conform to the principles set by Water For People.

Vested for Success

In November 2011, Water For People announced its goal of 100 percent coverage in Chinda had been reached. Community residents are very happy. Children now get up, bathe, get dressed, and scamper off to school instead of making the dangerous trek

Figure 7.1 Water for People Results as of 2010

Country Program	Water Systems Monitored	Water Systems Operational	Sustainability Percentage
Bolivia	91	87	96%
Guatemala	63	57	90%
Honduras	87	80	92%
India	275	271	99%
Malawi	137	130	95%

down the steep and rocky path to the river to fetch water. With easy access to clean water, people's dignity level is raised and overall health is improved. Celebrations are held when water openings occur. With a big smile, Castejon reported, "Once we even broke a bucket because we no longer needed to use it to get water from the river!"

However, the ultimate test is not getting the water flowing. Breslin defined success in this way: "When all the communities in the regions we work in are fully covered, when water and sanitation services expand as populations grow without our ongoing support, when money and technical support are in place to keep water flowing and sanitation services utilized forever, and when communities and regions no longer need us anymore. When this is achieved, we can leave an area knowing that they will be successful on their own. And we'll know we've influenced the sector when others replicate our work throughout communities and regions where we do not work directly. That's success!"

And when Water For People looks at the sustainability metrics, it sees progress. Independent monitoring reports that an average of 96 percent of its water systems are still functioning after four years.

INTEGRATED MANAGEMENT SYSTEMS

Dan Keto and Dean Dorcas met each other as midshipmen at the United States Naval Academy in 1987. It was an instant bond.

Although they began their careers in the Navy, both knew that one day they wanted to follow the American dream of running their own businesses. As their military duties came to an end, the pair bandied about potential business ventures. Dan was more a strategist; Dean was very focused and disciplined. The two young entrepreneurs decided to join forces and began investigating potential businesses that did not require much capital.

The idea came up to start a staffing firm. Dan explained, "It seemed like a good idea—we both had a knack for managing people."[9] Their research indicated that the industry was growing rapidly and still maintained decent gross margins. They also found succeeding would take more hard work than capital—with the biggest hurdle getting new customers and recruiting workers.

Believing that being a little different from other staffing firms would give them a competitive advantage, they decided to offer local businesses administrative and white-collar-type work using a "senior" workforce. The rationale? Seniors would be more reliable and consistent—something the men felt would be valuable to both potential customers and to their company. Senior Staffing, Inc., was born in 1996 in Seattle, Washington.

Dan and Dean's idea to staff senior workers seemed logical, but they soon realized a flaw in their logic. "We quickly found out that most companies in the Seattle area wanted workers with strong computer skills—which our senior workforce often didn't have," explained Dean. So the men did what smart entrepreneurs do: They followed the market and shifted to staffing their senior workforce in light industrial jobs, such as manufacturing, packaging, and assembly. "This was problematic as well—because potential customers didn't think older workers could be productive in more manual jobs."

Dan and Dean have always thought of themselves as innovative—constantly challenging themselves to find different and better ways to do things. So they approached a potential customer in the retail industry that was using about ten temporary workers every day to bag and tag clothing. To win the business, they came up with a creative value proposition. "Rather than simply 'staff' workers and charge the typical markup, we went to the customer with the idea for him to 'outsource' the work to Senior Staffing for 5 percent less than what they were currently paying. We thought if we could guarantee our client a cost savings and we took the risk of getting the workers to do the same work faster, we'd have a better chance of winning the work," Dan explained. "Now our challenge would be to motivate our workers to do the job faster than the previous company who typically had workers half the age of our workers."

Dan and Dean went to work—but not on getting out the bullwhip. Instead they studied how the work was being done. Could it be streamlined? Could they eliminate non–value-added activities? Could they teach slower workers to work as fast as the best workers? The duo developed team-based tracking and incentive programs to track productivity and motivate employees. "We believed if the group of ten worked cohesively as a team, they could achieve significant productivity gains. We did the math and established productivity targets. If the workers could increase their productivity, we would share some of our extra profits with them. Our goal was to create a win-win situation with our employees—where the more we won, the more they won with extra dollars in their pockets."

Sam Burke was the operations manager for the retailer at the time, and he remembers Dan and Dean's offer clearly. "I thought they were nuts. Here were these two young guys telling me their senior workers could do manual work faster than the temps we had that were than half their age. But I thought what the heck. They guaranteed me a 5 percent cost reduction, so I thought I would try them out." To Sam's surprise, Senior Staffing was able to improve per-hour productivity by over 40 percent. Sam was so impressed that he joined Dan and Dave to help them grow their company.

The success led Dan and Dean to rename the company Integrated Management Systems Inc. (IMS) because they felt strongly that their agency should be far more than a body shop; rather it should offer brainpower in helping companies be more productive in solving their production needs. IMS grew rapidly and was named one of the fastest-growing companies in Washington State three different times.

Unfortunately, Dan and Dean learned a hard lesson along the way. "One of the biggest challenges IMS has faced with our approach is that it has been a victim of its own operational success," Dan explained. "Customers usually do not realize how inefficient their operations are. IMS sometimes has been able to increase overall productivity by over 300 percent. When it priced the work at 5 percent below previous costs, a 300 percent increase in output created very substantial profit margins for the company. At first customers were ecstatic with the productivity gains, but then they realized that all of the benefit after the 5 percent guaranteed savings was going into IMS's profit. This led to customer resentment or opened the door for competition to undercut the business on price. IMS has lost business because of this."

Dean agreed. "While IMS was successful, at the end of the day the results were not really fair and balanced for our customers. We won a lot—and they only won 5 percent. In today's hypercompetitive business environment, customers often forget where they were and want to know what you've done for them lately. We realized IMS needed a long-term value model with our customers and began taking a Vested approach with them in regard to sharing in efficiency gains and cost savings."

In 2006, IMS got a big break—landing a contract for 200 warehouse workers. The company invested in developing software and productivity tracking tools that could scale to such large environments. Once again, it was a huge hit.

Figure 7.2 IMS 1 To 3 Year Comparison of Results for Client "X"

	Prior to IMS	After 1 Year	After 3 Years
Customer Benefits			
Unit labor cost	$237 per container	$175 per container	$150 per container
Cases per hour processed	146 cases per hour	300 cases per hour	>420 cases per hour
Employee turnover	Average 70 days on job (>50% turnover per mo.)	Average 180 days on job (<10% turnover per mo.)	Average 380 days on job (<5% turnover per mo.)
Quality rating	Last in network of 6 operations	Occasionally first in network	Consistently first in network
Employee Benefits			
Employee wage	$8.75 per hour (temporary labor wage)	$11.50 per hour ($9.25 base with bonus pay)	$13.00 per hour ($9.25 base with bonus pay)
IMS Profit Benefits			
Gross profit/ EBITDA	5% / 1%	20% / 5%	25% / 10%

Karl Koehler, who joined IMS in 2005 as a partner and, subsequently became chief operating officer, points to the power the Vested approach can bring by sharing the three-year results for one of IMS's largest clients in the above figure. At this operation, IMS workers unload shipping containers and repack the product into outbound trailers that are headed to different parts of the country.

Karl pointed to the fact that Vested deals can—and do— work not just with small teams of ten; they also work with large teams. "Traditional temporary staffing margins for high-volume warehousing operations range from 5 percent to 10 percent on the very high end, and they hope to achieve EBITDA [earnings before interest, taxes, depreciation, and amortization] of 1 percent. With IMS's Vested approach, our business model is structured around 25 percent gross margins with an EBITDA of 10 percent.

At first, customers think this is too high. But then they realize we use much of these higher margins to invest back into their business to make further improvements.

"The Vested approach keeps the employees, IMS management, and our client all aligned with the same priorities. We have developed sophisticated tracking and monitoring tools and processes to ensure we are all in sync with performance against goals. We all have the same goals, and when we achieve these goals, there are clear incentives for each of the three groups."

Dean is very happy with the results. "IMS has been very successful by applying a long-term, Vested approach with our clients. We've been able to move from a Seattle-based firm staffing small to midsize operations with a handful of workers to providing national operations with over 200 workers in some locations. Today the company continues to expand its outsourcing model around the United States and has also commercialized its software technology into a product called Easy Metrics which, using the same IMS methodology, has helped its customers increase their productivity by over 40 percent on average."

Dan, Dean, and Karl are steadfast in how they define winning in business. "Today, we seek a balanced three-way win between IMS's profits, employee incentive pay, and savings for our customers," explained Karl. "We deeply believe in a Vested approach. We run our entire business using the principles of Vested."

THE DIVERSEY AND WIPRO (R)EVOLUTION

In 2005, Diversey, a leading global provider of commercial cleaning, sanitation, and hygiene solutions, found itself in a very difficult situation. Faced with heavy debt and flat sales, a new chief financial officer launched a mandate that tasked Diversey's information technology (IT) organization to lower the company's IT spending from about 5 percent cost as percentage of sales to 2.5 percent. Diversey decided that outsourcing a large portion of IT with an offshore partner was the only way to reach the aggressive financial target. When chief information officer (CIO) Matt Peterson signed his first outsourcing agreement, his first goal was cost reduction: "And it was a long way down the list to get to No. 2."[10]

It was definitely not a Vested relationship.

In 2006, Diversey signed a five-year, $100 million+ outsourcing agreement with Wipro, a global IT service provider. Diversey used a classic lift-and-shift approach to turn over most of its existing IT processes to Wipro. The plan paid off. By year 2 of the five-year deal, Wipro had delivered the desired financial and organizational targets. Former CIO Peterson claimed success in an interview with *InformationWeek* in March 2009. He proudly pointed out that Diversey's outsourcing agreement with Wipro had given him and his team the ability to change "from efficient order-takers to actual strategic business enablers in the company's growth and development."[11]

The Second Generation: Transformation

With success under their belt, both parties were ready to embark on the next leg of their journey and work with Diversey managers on strategic new projects. The companies turned to end customers and the business groups for guidance. Throughout 2009, a joint Diversey/Wipro team conducted interviews and surveys to get both subjective and objective feedback. Interviews with key stakeholders and users revealed that the current outsourced IT support model faced many challenges similar to those that confront typical manufacturing value chains. These include reducing backlogs, achieving consistent quality, continuously improving process efficiencies, scheduling preventive maintenance, work prioritization, and achieving proper metrics.

With cost savings conquered and major changes ahead, the logical next step was a contract extension to adjust the agreement to focus on new priorities. Chris Windsor, Diversey's director of vendor management, led the development of the new contract. He explained, "The resulting agreement was a natural evolution and enhancement of the original model."

Wipro set out to deliver on its promise of standardizing legacy IT processes globally and transforming IT from a cost center to a group that creates value for Diversey business units. The goal was to leverage technology to automate repetitive activities and thus reduce costs, improve productivity, and increase quality. Diversey and Wipro committed to dynamic service levels that adjust over the contract term for optimal results, and they revised key metrics based on business needs to meet objectives—not just measuring activities.

Getting the metrics right was a big lesson the Diversey IT team learned the hard way. "In the first engagement with Wipro, the IT team was deeply involved in setting detailed SLAs [service-level agreements], but leaders from other parts of the business were not," Windsor said. "As a result, Diversey's IT group was meeting its SLAs, but the company overall was not getting full value in customer-satisfaction surveys. The big aha? What our IT team thought was important *wasn't necessarily important to our customers.*"

Standardization and increased service levels were key elements, but they were only half of the challenge for Diversey. Both parties wanted to go beyond standardization. They wanted to create a competitive advantage in terms of cost and service by identifying and deploying transformation projects, such as cloud-based technology platforms that allow for a collaborative working environment and maintain business continuity. The execution of cloud computing strategies reduced the company's carbon footprint by eliminating ten company servers and decreased the need for business travel and the purchase of hardware and software. The initiative helped Diversey reduce its carbon dioxide emissions by 73 metric tons.

The effort earned industry recognition, including that of Google. Dave Girouard, president of enterprise for Google, expressed his excitement. "Diversey's efforts to cut their carbon emissions while growing their business is a model for sustainable IT. This recognition [of success] is well deserved and reinforces the environmental benefits of cloud computing."

The dual-prong approach to standardize repetitive process and drive transformation projects paid off. "The results speak for themselves," Brett Hoag, Diversey's CIO, explained. Third-party benchmarking by RampRate, a leading IT sourcing adviser, revealed that the Diversey/Wipro combination was in the twenty-seventh percentile, meaning that Diversey is paying less than 73 percent of all companies for the same performance levels.

With an IT scorecard that was consistently "green," the parties sought to move to the third phase of transformation: a strategy designed to better link the services Wipro performs directly to business value.

The Third Generation: Vesting for Success in the Qwest for Value

"We wanted to shift the focus and make IT an enabler to the business," explained Hoag. "Our vision was that business units would be able to pay as you go for the services they wanted, when they wanted, at service levels they wanted and valued. If we could do this, we felt IT would be seen as adding value to the business versus being an overhead expense."

As the parties embarked on the third leg of their outsourcing journey, they wanted to make sure they incorporated best practices. During their research, they heard about the University of Tennessee's "Deal Review" process. "Both Diversey and Wipro felt that we were doing all the right things, but we wanted to make sure we had all the pieces of the puzzle in place to motivate both parties to most effectively achieve our desired outcomes," Hoag said. Werner Graf, Wipro's U.S. general manager of consumer products, agreed. "The timing was perfect as we were just beginning our third-generation efforts."

Diagnosis: Good . . . and on the Way to Great

With both parties full of passion and feeling success, the time was right to take their relationship to the next level. The companies decided to conduct a Vested Outsourcing deal review to understand how to improve all aspects of their relationship—ranging from the contract itself, pricing model, governance structure, and trust levels. The deal review revealed that both companies were well on their way to a Vested relationship and that the parties had high levels of trust. The review also assessed the Diversey/Wipro relationship against ten essential elements outlined in *The Vested Outsourcing Manual*.[12]

The assessment gave insight into areas where Diversey and Wipro needed to focus. The team had a strong governance structure and impressive strategic alignment. Long-term C-level engagements were established and drove mutual benefits and value for both parties. However, the deal review found that there was not a unified clear vision and that desired outcomes were only informally documented. The existing relationship, while stressing transformation, focused on the "now" in terms of a traditional statement of work. This is a common mistake, and one that can easily anchor a service provider in the present rather than focusing on the future.

The deal review also showed weaknesses in the pricing model. The Diversey/Wipro deal focused solely on SLA penalties, which is common in IT outsourcing. Such a focus is effective at driving performance against SLAs, but it does not set the stage properly to incentivize Wipro to make the necessary investments to achieve transformation.

Moving from Now to Next

Kiran Vedak, chief technology officer at Diversey, was glad the Diversey/Wipro team participated in the deal review process. "We are not surprised by the findings of the deal review. We knew there were opportunities. The process helped us to see the shortcomings clearly in front of us and get a sense of urgency to address them."

First on the list for the joint Diversey/Wipro team was development of a formalized shared vision. "When you stop and think about it, a shared vision is a very powerful guiding beacon. We began crafting our shared vision within days after getting our deal review diagnostic," Hoag said. The results? A formally documented vision that both companies could rally around:

> Dynamically innovate and collaborate to provide information
> technology services that transform our industry. Together, we
> deliver measureable benefits and mutual competitive advantage
> for our ecosystem of people, partners and customers.

"Our shared vision is straightforward yet powerful," Wipro's Graf explained. "Simply creating the shared vision and desired outcomes created a great deal of energy as a team."

The Next Generation: The Journey to Vested

Together, Diversey and Wipro have come a long way since signing their initial outsourcing agreement in 2005. In less than five short years, Diversey's IT group has gone from old school and expensive to nimble, cost effective, and green. In September 2010, Diversey was listed by *InformationWeek* as one of the top 10 U.S. manufacturers that are leading innovative deployment of IT. Overall, Diversey was among the top 200 companies recognized for technology innovation in the world. The National Outsourcing Association named the pair the IT Outsourcing Project of the Year in November 2011. The association's awards recognize and reward innovation and achievement by suppliers, users, and integrated teams within the outsourcing industry.

But what does 2012 bring? Announcement came in 2011 that Sealed Air, a company well known for its bubble wrap product, would purchase Diversey. But the impending sale did not halt progress. Hoag and his team—with Wipro right alongside them—continued to march forward. "The Vested Outsourcing deal review process also highlighted something that is crucial to our success within the next year—the importance of having a contract with a flexible framework. Sealed Air is currently acquiring Diversey and, although Sealed Air uses Wipro as their service provider, you never know what the future will bring. We set out to structure our agreement as flexible, and it has stood the test of time. Both parties are able to respond effectively to changes in the business," Hoag stated.

Werner Graf echoed Hoag's sentiments. "As Diversey enters into a period of known unknowns, I can't think of two better components to have—a flexible contractual framework and a trusting business relationship. At the end of the day, this team will be able to accomplish whatever the business demands."

ONE SIZE DOES FIT ALL

From burgers to bridges to small businesses and even not-for-profits, the Vested Five Rules are universal rules that have the power to transform any organization. What started as a research project seven years ago has proven to be rules that organizations—no matter what size or mission—can rely on if they are seeking true change and transformation.

CONCLUSION

I took the road less traveled by, and that has made all the difference.

—*Robert Frost*

STARTING A VESTED (R)EVOLUTION

We began by saying that the purpose of this book was to share the stories and secrets behind some of world's most successful business relationships. We shared how the best of the best approach working with others to unlock a powerful motivating force for their business partners to deliver transformational results. We also set out to provide a framework to challenge your thinking and help you redefine your own business relationships to make them more successful.

We profiled McDonald's—which created a System to be reckoned with over 50 years ago and has embedded Vested thinking in the very fabric of its most strategic supplier relationships. And we covered Diversey and Wipro, which believe it is never too late to find a better way to approach an existing relationship.

We have shown that Vested thinking works not only in large corporations but also in state and local governments, nonprofits, and small businesses.

We have shown that the Vested rules can be applied to virtually any type of relationships, not just supplier relationships. Vested thinking works for forging partnerships with outsourced service providers to improve service and lower costs for back-office procure to pay, global facilities management, and contract manufacturing. It also works for developing political agreements with groups such as parent–teacher associations. And it enables McDonald's to create a competitive advantage in what many would think of as pure commodities of buying beef and baked goods.

WHICH PATH DO YOU CHOOSE?

Innovation and breakthrough results are often a key focus of an organization's strategy. Most organizations fail to embrace the fact that often they must rely on the expertise of those beyond their four walls. Unfortunately, Vested relationships are not the norm. We hope you can use these stories of the most successful Vested relationships to help your organization understand the power of applying the Vested principles to your relationships.

We also want to remind you that a Vested approach is a choice.

We challenge you to choose the Vested way the next time you find yourself searching for a desired outcome that seems out of reach. We challenge you to think through how you can apply the Five Rules of Vested Outsourcing in your organization and move beyond merely saying "partnership" to actually creating Vested relationships that have the power to unlock innovation and drive transformation for your organization—whether it is a Fortune 500 company seeking a competitive advantage in a dog-eat-dog world, a small business seeking creative ways to build business alliances or forge deeper relationships with clients, or a nonprofit organization trying to change the world.

As you embark on your Vested relationships, ask yourself these questions:

Are you willing to focus on outcomes and not transactions? Are you willing to allow someone outside of your four walls come up with the best solution?

Can you describe what you want without describing how to do it?

Can you define and measure outcomes you hope to obtain? How will these measures be calculated? Who will be responsible for them?

How will you develop a dynamic pricing model? Are you willing to share the wealth when you are successful? Do you have properly aligned incentives that motivate organizations and individuals to deliver transformative results?

Are you willing to develop a governance structure that provides insight into the relationship instead of oversight?

Of course, not all of these questions can be answered right away. But you will need to answer them correctly as you follow the path to Vested.

We hope you choose to join the Vested (R)evolution.

Join at www.VestedWay.com.

EPILOGUE

A meme is an idea that behaves like a virus—that moves through
a population, taking hold in each person it infects.

—*Malcolm Gladwell*

Throughout the evolution of our research leading experts and innovators have contributed to the development of Vested principles and the adoption of the Vested business model in nearly every industry and business function. The story of how the Vested movement came to be is itself an example of how Vested relationships lead to new opportunities and mutual success.

As we conducted our research, it quickly became apparent that the principles we were uncovering were not applicable to just outsourcing. In fact, our methodology has a transformative potential that can rival that of Lean and Six Sigma, well-known business management philosophies used to reach operational excellence. The Vested methodology can reach across all industries and markets and create sweeping changes in how business is done.

Along with this realization came a big challenge. The business world typically does not adopt or embrace academic research. Instead, great research often remains trapped inside university walls and bureaucracy. Most business professionals have not even heard of the Nobel Prize–winning research of Dr. Oliver Williamson in transaction cost economics (which we reference often), although it introduces foundational concepts that would greatly impact all business transactions and contracts.

As we explored this dilemma, Kate and Dr. Alex Miller, then associate dean of the University of Tennessee's Center for Executive Education, came to realize that we could take the new methodology based on our research and apply it to the challenge of getting Vested recognized and adopted. Just as McDonald's created a System, we wanted to create a Vested ecosystem that would expand the research across all industries. By creating key Vested relationships with individuals from both academic and private sectors, we believed, we could expand our methodology to enable its widespread adoption even as it continues to evolve. Vested still could be studied by academics and, at the same time, be positioned to become a new business model.

It was a radical idea.

With this strategy in mind, we formed the first Vested relationship with Elizabeth Kanna, a business producer who specializes in taking concepts and positioning them as compelling brands that evolve into movements that drive adoption. After studying our research, she coined a name—Vested—that spoke to the heart of the principles we had outlined. From there, she developed an integrated, constantly evolving, branding and market adoption strategy. She also introduced us to Palgrave Macmillan, the publisher of Jim Womak's pioneering book *LEAN: The Machine That Changed the World* and the publishing home for our Vested book series.

Drawing on the concepts in Malcolm Gladwell's book *The Tipping Point*, we decided that Vested had everything necessary to become a dynamic, sustainable *movement*.

Movements are powerful vehicles that bring about sweeping changes and spread a concept much further than traditional marketing practices. They inspire passion and are focused on win-win results (just as the core principle of Vested is that only by working together toward mutual goals can both parties in a relationship reach their desired outcomes).

Along with Karl Manrodt and Mike Ledyard, Kate began traveling the globe, teaching and speaking to spread the Vested movement, first in the outsourcing and supply chain verticals and then to other industry sectors. Individuals in both the academic and the private sectors have worked tirelessly, and often at their own expense, to bring Vested to nearly every industry and business function.

The book you hold in your hands is the result of the University of Tennessee's Center for Executive Education daring to be innovative and creating Vested partnerships in order to drive academic research into a dynamic movement that can empower *your* company, organization, or partnership for success you cannot even imagine (yet). We hope our message will not sit as just another business book upon your shelf, but that it will be a catalyst to a transformational, profitable future.

The Vested movement will continue to evolve and expand even beyond our initial vision for rivaling Lean and Six Sigma. Why? Because Vested relationships create wins that would not be possible otherwise—and those successes create more successes.

ACKNOWLEDGMENTS

No matter what accomplishments you make, somebody helped you.

—*Althea Gibson*

This book is the product of seven years of research into outsourcing as a business practice. Our initial work led us to study some of the world's most successful business agreements. As we pause to formally write down our thank-yous, it is with great pleasure that we recognize that the spirit of collaboration was embedded into our research from the onset. To say this book is "by Kate and Karl" would be misleading. Without significant contributions made by other people, especially Jeanne Kling, this book simply would not exist.

We would like to start by highlighting the University of Tennessee's Center for Executive Education, where Kate is a faculty member. Dr. Alex Miller—associate dean of the center at the time of the initial research—and Kate were adamant that the university reach out to collaborate with the best minds in academia, industry, and government. Karl—a professor at Georgia Southern University—joined the research team at the outset to add his expertise in performance measurement. Mike Ledyard, while not part of this particular book effort, was part of the original research team. We are also grateful for support from Dr. Matt Myers, Dr. Ted Stank, Carolyn Cuddy, Bric Wheeler, Karen Hanlon, and Dr. Chad Autry.

Next, we want to thank the funders of our original research. Our first benefactors were Boeing, Lockheed Martin, Northrop Grumman, Pratt & Whitney, and General Electric, all of which contributed to our research fund. These funds helped the research team collect and share best-practice techniques in performance-based contracting. Our work expanded when the United States Air Force funded a large research project to study best practices in buying services. This was our opportunity to study some of the world's most successful outsourcing relationships.

With support and funds, we set out on a journey during which we worked with over 50 organizations. We recruited experts in various fields to help us test the concepts of Vested in a wide range of industries and services. Simply put, we created an extended field-based research team that enabled us to create and test our diagnostic tools in real companies. Did the Vested Five Rules make sense? And, most importantly, would they work in various industries?

Like the early days of Wikipedia development, passionate people came together—some volunteering hundreds of hours—to rally around the desire to help to build a movement for a better way to do business. In all, our "extended family" of Vested Outsourcing field researchers and program faculty included more than 50 highly talented and passionate people who deeply believe that Vested is the defining approach for business relationships in the twenty-first century, including renowned business producer Elizabeth Kanna, who helped us formulate the vision to help shift Vested from research to a formidable movement in business.

A few of these experts joined us as program faculty in our performance-based service acquisition courses for the Air Force as well as our Vested Outsourcing courses. Others have helped us write white papers or case studies tailored to specific industries or services. And still others have become experts in the Vested principles and actively coach companies as Vested Outsourcing certified deal architects. And four individuals—Mike Ledyard, Jacqui Crawford, Jeanette Nyden, and Katherine Kawamoto—joined us as coauthors when we wrote our first two books on the topic of Vested.

We'd like to recognize these individuals for participating in our original research and/or joining us as part of our executive education faculty teaching in our Air Force or Vested Outsourcing executive education courses:

Steve Brady
Stu Cranston
Bill DiBenedetto
Lyle Eesley
Bonnie Keith
Jeanne Kling
Mike Ledyard
Pete Moore
Jeanette Nyden
Steve Symmes

These consulting firms and lawyers have helped us develop and vet our methodologies, test, and deploy our tools and methodologies in the field with real companies:

Capto Consulting	Tracy Currie
Baker and McKenzie	Ed Hansen, Michael Mensik, Peter George
The Forefront Group	Bruce Allen, Michele Coquis, Angela Easterwood, Bonnie Keith, Donna Massari, Shelley Pilsbury, and Huahai Wei

J. Nyden and Co.	Jeanette Nyden
SPOT Consulting	Kim Keating and Alton Martin
Supply Chain Visions	Ralph Datoc, Steve Geary,
	Adrianne Gross, Mike Ledyard,
	Pete Moore, Steve Murray,
	Mark Nassutti, Steve Symmes,
	Joe Tillman, and Astrid Uka
HP	George Kimball
Sutherland	Jim Groton

In addition, nonprofit and professional associations, industry analysts and academics have supported and helped us expand our work with collaborative research and development of white papers:

ARC Advisory Group/Adelante
Center for Outsource Research and Education
Corporate Executive Board
International Association for Contract and Commercial
  Management
The Sourcing Interest Group

We offer special gratitude to Richard Wilding of the Cranfield School of Business, Dr. Jerry Ledlow of Georgia Southern University, and Dr. John Grant (retired) of the University of California—Berkeley.

We are particularly indebted to the companies that are profiled in this book. A special thank you to the folks who helped us tell wonderful stories of how you are applying Vested. We conducted extensive interviews in these companies in order to capture the story of their Vested journeys. The individual quotes found within the book, unless noted differently, were generated within the interview process.

P&G's Game Changer in Outsourcing

P&G	Larry Bridge, Julie DeSylva, Lydia Jacobs-Horton, Bill Metz, William Reeves
Jones Lang LaSalle	Patricia Becker, Elizabeth Brown, Thomas Browne, Peter Bulgarelli, Joanna Duker, Colin Dyer, Heidi Fulcher, Todd Hamiter, Cindy Hill, Tim McParlane, Lauralee Martin, Kathryn Nice, Yvonne Peterson, Charlie Petit, Jim Redmond, Teresa Reis, Sylvia Rojas, William Thummel, Kelly Yates
Compass Group USA	Frank Lombardi

Minnesota Turns I-35W Bridge Tragedy into Triumph

Minnesota Department of Transportation	Jon Chiglo, Kevin Gutknecht
Flatiron Manson	Peter Sanderson
FIGG Engineering	Linda Figg
University of Minnesota	Catherine French

U.S. Department of Energy Transforms Weapons Wasteland to Wildlife Site

CH2M Hill	Melody Ambrose, John Corsi, Denny Ferrera, Scott Haskins, Elisa Speranza, Nancy Tuor

Microsoft and Accenture Perfect a Pricing Model

Microsoft	Henric Häggquist, Taylor Hawes, Srini Krishna, Tim McBride, Mike Simms

Accenture   Andrew Cheung, Patricia Humphrey, Mike Salvino, Gil Wootton, Joseph Wright

McDonald's Secret Sauce for Supply Chain Success

McDonald's   Jose-Luis Bretones-Lopez, Francesca DeBiase, Kim Dziewinski, Bruce Feinberg, Dan Gorsky, Artemis Hiss, Gary Johnson, Jerome Lyman, Denise Martin, Zoran Rancic, Linda Rasmussen Horacio Sbolla

McDonald's Suppliers

Armada Supply Chain Solutions	John Burke
Baldwin-Richardson Foods	Brad Kirk, Eric Johnson, Jill Wiabe
The Bama Companies Inc.	S. Bailey, Mark J. Bendix
Cargill	Neli Garcia, Stephen Guinta, Pete Richter
Danaco Solutions, LLC	Carey Cooper, Saretta Kessler
Dean Foods	Stephanie Ashley, Midd McManus
Fresh Start Bakeries	Russ Doll, Denise Ramos, Mike Ward
Havi Global Solutions USA	Kim Belehradek, Dan Musachia
Keystone Foods	Jerry Dean
Klosterman Bakeries	Chip Klosterman, Debbie Elliot
Lopez Foods	Bekki Liles, Ed Sanchez
Martin-Brower	Greg Nickele, Betty Williams

Mullins Foods	Jeanne Gannon, Mike Mullins
OSI Group	Kevin Scott, Mike Boccio, Kristina Swanson
Simplot	Becky Busch, Karin Hart
Tyson Foods	Devin Cole, Patty Richardson

Water For People Case Study

CH2MHill	Eileen Lambert, Elisa Spiranza
Water For People	Ned Breslin, Susan Davis, Katja Neubauer, John Sauer

Integrated Management Systems

Dean Dorcas, Dan Keto, Karl Koehler

How Diversey and Wipro are (R)evolutionizing IT

Diversey	Sarah Alt, Brett Hoag, Sarah Lange, Matt Peterson, Colin Ryder, Robert Tracey, Kiran Vedak, Chris Windsor
Wipro	Somjit Amrit, David Anderson, Jeffrey Dymm, Werner Graf, Madhavan Seshadri Rangaprasad

Last, we would like to recognize special people in our lives. A formal thank you for Mike Watts, Rhonda Watts, Laurie Hanley, and Karen Wiley: You keep Kate organized, on time, and everything running in perfect order for her. You are a savior for Kate, and for that we are all indebted. Finally, the best for last. We are indebted to our spouses—Greg Picinich, Susie Manrodt, and Steve Kling. You have shown us that the Vested principles apply even to marriages. We could not be happier being Vested with you.

NOTES

INTRODUCTION

1. The Inside Up Outsourcing Connection, "How Vested Outsourcing Is Changing the Way Companies Do Business," January 6, 2012, http://insideup.com/blogs/b2bsourcing/2012/01/06/how-vested-outsourcing-is-changing-the-way-companies-do-business/.

CHAPTER 1: VESTING FOR SUCCESS

1. Former P&G CEO A. G. Lafley profiled P&G's philosophies in his book (with R. Charan), *The Game Changer* (New York: Crown Business, 2008).
2. Quoted in Michael Bloch and Elizabeth C. Lempres, "From Internal Service Provider to Strategic Partner: An Interview with the Head of Global Business Services at P&G. Filippo Passerini Is Bringing the Back Office into the Boardroom," *McKinsey Quarterly* (July 2008).
3. Assertions from Len Ackland, *Making a Real Killing: Rocky Flats and the Nuclear West* (Albuquerque: University of New Mexico Press, 1999).
4. U. S. General Accounting Office, Report to Congress, "Nuclear Cleanup: Progress Made at Rocky Flats, but Closure by 2006 Is Unlikely, and Costs May Increase," February 2001, http://www.gao.gov/new.items/d01284.pdf.
5. U.S. Department of Energy, "Rocky Flats Closure Legacy: Accelerated Closure Concept," http://rockyflats.apps.em.doe.gov/chapters/01%20-%20Accelerated%20Closure.pdf.
6. Dan Charles, "Will These Lands Ne'er Be Cleaned?" *New Scientist* no. 1670 (June 24, 1989). DOE completed a revised baseline in 1996 based on Congress's directive to accelerate work. The 1996 life cycle cost estimate for the environmental management program at Rocky Flats was $17.3 billion, 52 percent less than the 1995 life cycle cost estimate of $36.6 billion, after taking FY 1995 expenditures into account. The $19.0 billion reduction in the program's estimated life cycle cost reflects site-wide changes in work scope and facility operation schedules. These

changes were in response to Recommendation 94–1 of the Defense Nuclear Facilities Safety Board and the DOE's Plutonium Vulnerability Assessment, which required that the consolidation, stabilization, and repackaging of vulnerable materials be accelerated. The accelerated schedules dictated near-term, site-specific reprioritization efforts to redirect resources from other site programs to plutonium stabilization and related risk-reduction activities. These changes emphasized early action, reduction in waste generation, and modifications to waste management strategies. The revised baseline estimated completion in 2065—10 years earlier than the 1995 projections. U.S. Department of Energy, "Environmental Management: Rocky Flats Environmental Technology site 2," n.d. http://www.em.doe.gov/bemr/BEMRSites/rfts2.aspx.

7. Michael E. Long, "Half Life—The Lethal Legacy of America's Nuclear Waste," *National Geographic* 202, no. 1 (January 2002): 1–33. Available at http://science.nationalgeographic.com/science/earth/inside-the-earth/nuclear-waste/#page=10.

8. A 2006 postproject Government Accounting Office (GAO) report said the actual total cost of cleanup was $10 billion, with $7.7 billion for Kaiser-Hill. The contract and project started in 1995 and were completed in 2005. GAO Report to Congressional Requesters, "Nuclear Cleanup of Rocky Flats: DOE Can Use Lessons Learned to Improve Oversight of Other Sites' Cleanup," July 2006, http://rockyflats.apps.em.doe.gov/references/185 GAO%20RF%20Lessons%20Learned%202006–352.pdf.

CHAPTER 2: P&G'S GAME CHANGER IN OUTSOURCING

1. Kate Vitasek and Mike Ledyard, *Vested Outsourcing: Five Rules That Will Transform Outsourcing* (New York: Palgrave Macmillan, 2010). Chapter 3 outlines 10 Ailments that commonly plague outsourcing agreements. They include the power of not doing, measuring minutiae, driving blind, the zero-sum game, sandbagging, honeymoon effect, junkyard dog factor, activity trap, outsourcing paradox, and penny wise and pound foolish.

2. GBS consolidated internal services such as finance, accounting, employee services, customer logistics, purchasing, and information technology into a single global organization providing services to all P&G business units.

3. Quoted in Chris Murphy, "Procter & Gamble CIO Filippo Passerini: 2010 Chief of the Year," *Information Week Global CIO*, December 4, 2010. http://www.informationweek.com/news/global-cio/interviews/show Article.jhtml?articleID=228500182.

4. Quoted in Michael Bloch and Elizabeth C. Lempres, "From Internal Service Provider to Strategic Partner: An Interview with the Head of Global Business Services at P&G. Filippo Passerini Is Bringing the Back Office into the Boardroom," *McKinsey Quarterly* (July 2008).

5. Thomas J. DeLong, David L. Ager, Warren Brackin, Alex Cabanas, and Phil Shellhammer, "Case Study: Procter & Gamble: Global Business Services," Harvard Business School, June 18, 2004, Product # 404124-PDF-ENG.

6. Quoted in Bloch and Lempres, "From Internal Service Provider to Strategic Partner."
7. Excerpted from internal Jones Lang Lasalle Power Point document, "Shared Vision from FM Outsourcing Agreement," no individual author listed.
8. Personal interview with Lauralee Martin by Kate Vitasek, Karl Manrodt, and Jeanne Kling, February 18, 2011.
9. Personal interview with William Reeves by Kate Vitasek, Karl Manrodt, and Jeanne Kling at P&G headquarters, May 12, 2011.
10. P&Gers frequently refer to PVP-driven decisions. PVP stands for the principles, values, and purpose that define ethics and mandate behavior.
11. P&G Internal Document—CoreNet PowerPoint Presentation, Corporate Real Estate 2010, New Models for Solutions Delivery, Procter & Gamble Case Study, 2004.
12. Quoted in Bloch and Lempres, "From Internal Service Provider to Strategic Partner."
13. Larry Bridge is also the 2 in a Box partner with Charlie Petit and Tim McParlane.
14. Personal interview with Larry Bridge by Kate Vitasek, Karl Manrodt, and Jeanne Kling at P&G headquarters, May 12, 2011.
15. Tim Venable, "Procter & Gamble's William Reeves Driving Leading-Edge Service Delivery," *CoreNet Leader,* March 2005.
16. P&G results were officially released to the University of Tennessee research team members in September 2011.
17. Personal interview with Lydia Jacobs-Horton by Kate Vitasek, Karl Manrodt, and Jeanne Kling at P&G headquarters, May 12, 2011.

CHAPTER 3: MINNESOTA TURNS I-35W BRIDGE
TRAGEDY INTO TRIUMPH

1. These fatigue design rules were substantially improved as a result of research at Lehigh University in the 1970s.
2. Except for 1999, when MnDOT admitted submitting the wrong data.
3. Personal interview with Jon Chiglo, MnDOT project manager, by Jeanne Kling, February 4, 2011.
4. To adhere to the 2001 law, MnDOT carefully outlined the performance criteria for how it would select a contractor. Because MnDOT clearly documented the weighting criteria, potential bidders could develop a proposal that would best align with MnDOT's desired outcomes. The contractor whose proposal scored the highest according to the weighted criteria would earn the award. MnDOT began by first seeking requests for qualifications (RFQs) from interested bidders. A technical review committee reviewed the RFQs and selected a short list of contractors to proceed to the second phase. After those contractors were selected, MnDOT issued an RFP with defined criteria for bids. There were three

parts to the bidding proposals: (1) Equal Employment Opportunities and Disadvantaged Business Enterprise proposal, (2) technical proposal, and (3) pricing proposal. Part 1 ensured that potential bidders complied with state and federal laws and policies; failure to do so would result in rejection acceptance of a contract. Bid proposals were then separated into two parts, a technical proposal and a price proposal. Different MnDOT teams independently evaluated and scored each part. Under the best value approach, MnDOT was required to award the project to the proposer with the lowest score, not the lowest price.

5. A. Cho, "Mixing Social and Structural Skills; Leaders Guided Historic Rebuild Project," ENR.com, January 7, 2009, retrieved December 21, 2010, http://enr.construction.com/people/awards/2009/0107-Peter Sanderson.asp.

6. Henry Fountain, "Concrete Is Remixed with Environment in Mind," *New York Times*, March 31, 2009, http://www.nytimes.com/2009/03/31/science /earth/31conc.html?pagewanted=1&_r=2.

7. Jim Foti, "He Brings World of Experience to Bridge Project," *StarTribune* (Minneapolis-St. Paul), November 24, 2007, http://projects.dot.state. mn.us/35wbridge/pdfs/StarTribune1.pdf.

8. FIATECH is a consortium of industries and companies that includes the leading providers of engineering, design, and construction services. It serves as a clearinghouse for breakthrough ideas—best practices, innovations, and creative solutions.

CHAPTER 4: U.S. DEPARTMENT OF ENERGY TRANSFORMS WEAPONS WASTELAND TO WILDLIFE SITE

1. Mutual assured destruction is a military doctrine that emerged at the end of the Kennedy administration. It reflects the idea that a population could best be protected by leaving it vulnerable so long as the other side faced comparable vulnerabilities. In short, whoever shoots first dies second.

2. Kim Cameron and Marc LaVine, *Making the Impossible Possible: Leading Extraordinary Performance: The Rocky Flats Story* (San Francisco: Berritt Koehler, 2006).

3. M. Obmascik, "Price of Peace," *Denver Post*, June 25, 2000.

4. Jeremy Karpatkin, quoted in the Maria Rogers Oral History Program, *Rocky Flats: Rocky Flats Oral History Collection*, A Collaboration of the Rocky Flats Cold War Museum and the Boulder Public Library Carnegie Library for local history. Abstract # OH 1380.

5. GAO report to Congress, "Nuclear Cleanup of Rocky Flats: DOE Can Use Lessons Learned to Improve Oversight of Other Sites' Cleanup Activities," July 2006, http://www.gao.gov/products/GAO-06-352.

6. Kim Cameron, Robert E. Quinn, Jeff DeGraff, and Anjan V. Thakor, *Competing Values in Organizations* (Northhampton, MA: Edgar Elgar, 2006); and Cameron and LaVine, *Making the Impossible Possible*.

7. Personal interview with Denny Ferrera by Kate Vitasek, Karl Manrodt, and Jeanne Kling, December 19, 2011.

8. Original estimates were disclosed in DOE, 1995 Baseline Environmental Management Report. Information was confirmed and updated in subsequent years' reports. "Rocky Flats Closure Legacy: Accelerated Closure Concept," http://rockyflats.apps.em.doe.gov/chapters/01%20-%20Accelerated%20Closure.pdf.
9. Dan Charles, "Will These Lands Ne'er Be Cleaned?" *New Scientist*, June 24, 1989. A revised life cycle cost baseline of $17.3 billion was completed by DOE in 1996 based on the direction from Congress to accelerate work. This estimate was 52 percent less than the 1995 life cycle cost estimate of $36.6 billion, after taking FY 1995 expenditures into account. The $19.0 billion reduction reflected site-wide changes in work scope and facility operation schedules. These changes were in response to Defense Nuclear Facilities Safety Board Recommendation 94–1 and the Department's Plutonium Vulnerability Assessment, which stipulated that the consolidation, stabilization, and repackaging of vulnerable materials be accelerated. The accelerated schedules dictated near-term, site-specific reprioritization efforts to redirect resources from other site programs to plutonium stabilization and related risk-reduction activities. These changes emphasized early action, reduction in waste generation, and modifications to waste management strategies. The revised baseline estimated completion in 2065, ten years earlier than the 1995 projections. DOE report accessed at http://www.em.doe.gov/bemr/BEMRSites/rfts2.aspx.
10. Kaiser-Hill operated under two innovative DOE contracting models at Rocky Flats. The first, awarded in 1995, was the first performance-based contract in DOE history. It paid the contractor only for specific units of verifiable work. The model was in sharp contrast to the common maintenance and operations contracts where contractor's fee was based on subjective performance criteria. See http://www.ch2m.com/corporate/services/decontamination_and_decommissioning/assets/ProjectPortfolio/rocky.pdf.
11. Personal interview with Nancy Tuor by Kate Vitasek, Karl Manrodt, and Jeanne Kling, December 15, 2011.
12. The official 1995 Environmental Baseline Report estimated cleanup to be $37 billion and would take up to 75 years. A 2006 postproject GAO report reported the actual cleanup total cost of cleanup at $10 billion, with $7.7 billion for Kaiser-Hill. The contract and project were started in 1995 and were completed in 2005. GAO report to Congress, "Nuclear Cleanup of Rocky Flats."
13. Cameron and LaVine, *Making the Impossible Possible*, 103.
14. Colorado Department of Health and Environment; Environmental Protection Agency; National Atomic Energy Commission.
15. Final Rocky Flats Cleanup, http://rockyflats.apps.em.doe.gov/references/003%20-RFCA%20Doc-FNLRFCA-All.pdfhttp://www.cnn.com/.
16. A picocurie is a trillionth of a curie, which is the amount of radioactivity in a gram of radium.
17. Kim Cameron, "Positively Deviant Organizational Performance and the Role of Leadership Values," *Journal of Values-Based Leadership* 1, http://

www.valuesbasedleadershipjournal.com/issues/vol1issue1/cameron.php; Cameron et al., *Competing Values in Organizations*, January 21, 2009.

18. *ABC Nightline News*, December 20, 1994.

19. GAO report to Congress, "Nuclear Cleanup of Rocky Flats." Refer to endnote # 7.

20. Personal interview with Nancy Tuor by Kate Vitasek, Karl Manrodt, and Jeanne Kling, December 15, 2011.

21. GAO report to Congress, "Nuclear Cleanup of Rocky Flats." Refer to endnote # 7.

22. Cameron and LaVine, *Making the Impossible Possible*.

23. Obtaining this contract was a direct result of Kaiser-Hill's prior performance, safety record, and development of an aggressive yet credible plan to close the site decades earlier and for billions of dollars less. See http://www.ch2m.com/corporate/services/decontamination_and _decommissioning/assets/ProjectPortfolio/rocky.pdf.

24. Cameron and LaVine, *Making the Impossible Possible*.

25. Quoted in Joe Fiorill, "Rocky Flats Cleanup Contract Called Model for Future Federal Efforts," *Government Executive*, November 15, 2005.

26. Statistics from "CH2M Hill Inc. (and the Kaiser-Hill Company)," http:// www.nationalcorruptionindex.org/pages/profile.php?profile_id=354 (last updated May 16, 2009); and GAO report to Congress, "Nuclear Cleanup of Rocky Flats."

27. Quoted in Terre Satterfield and Joshua Levin, "Risk Communication, Fugitive Values, and the Problem of Trade-offs: Diagnosing the Breakdown of Deliberative Processes," in B. Johnston (ed.), *Half-Lives and Half-Truths: Confronting the Radioactive Legacy of the Cold War* (Santa Fe: SAR Press, 2007).

28. Rik Getty, Technical Adviser, Rocky Flats Coalition of Local Governments, "Statistical Confidence as It Relates to Soil Sampling at Rocky Flats." See http://www.rockyflatssc.org/residual_contamination /IVV_Statistical_Confidence_white_paper_rev_1.pdf.

29. GAO report to Congress, "Nuclear Cleanup of Rocky Flats." Refer to endnote # 7.

30. "Chemical Decontamination of Gloveboxes and Tanks Improves Safety, Reduces TRU Waste," *Technology @ Rocky Flats*, http:// rockyflats.apps.em.doe.gov/references/126-Chemical%20Decon%20 of%20Gloveboxes.pdf.

31. PUT official post cleanup GAO report here.

32. Personal interview with Nancy Tuor by Kate Vitasek, Karl Manrodt, and Jeanne Kling, December 15, 2011.

33. Personal interview with Denny Ferrera with Kate Vitasek, Karl Manrodt, and Jeanne Kling, December 19, 2011.

34. The official 1995 Environmental Baseline Report estimated cleanup to be $37 billion and would take 75 years. A 2006 post project Government Accountabilities report reported the actual cleanup total cost of cleanup at $10b, with $7.7b for Kaiser-Hill. The contract and project was started

in 1995 and was completed in 2005. GAO report to Congress, "Nuclear Cleanup of Rocky Flats."

35. Quoted in Rocky Flats Closure Project, 2007 Nova Award Nomination 13, http://www.cif.org/awards/2007/13_-_Rocky_Flats_Closure_Project. pdf.

36. Maria Rogers Oral History Program, *Rocky Flats; Rocky Flats Oral History Collection*, transcript for Rocky Flats Activists, October 28, 2006, OH1441v.

37. Michael E. Long, "Half Life—The Lethal Legacy of America's Nuclear Waste," *National Geographic*. Article republished at http://science.nationalgeographic.com/science/earth/inside-the-earth/nuclear-waste/#page=4.

38. Quoted in John Corsi, "Kaiser-Hill Announces Physical Completion of Rocky Flats Cleanup," October 13, 2005, http://www.ch2m.com/corporate/news_room/news_story.asp?story_id=35.

39. GAO, *Nuclear Cleanup: Preliminary Results of the Review of the Department of Energy's Rocky Flats Closure Project*, September, 2005, http://www.gao.gov/new.items/d051044r.pdf.

CHAPTER 5: MICROSOFT AND ACCENTURE PERFECT A PRICING MODEL

1. We have seen Vested relationships with the margins on the base work as low as zero and transformation incentives yielding profit margins for the service provider in excess of 80 percent.

2. Kate Vitasek with Jacqui Crawford, Jeanette Nyden, and Katherine Kawamoto, *The Vested Outsourcing Manual* (New York: Palgrave MacMillan, 2011), 143.

3. M. M. Sathyanarayan, *Offshoring Development: Proven Strategies and Tactics for Success* (Cupertino, CA: Globaldev Publishing, 2003); Robert Mottley, "Follow the Software: How Microsoft Outsourced Everything but Product Design," *American Shipper*, June 1, 1997.

4. Excerpt from site program documentation provided by Microsoft as part of case study research.

5. Oliver Williamson, "Outsourcing: Transaction Cost Economics and Supply Chain Management," *Journal of Supply Chain Management* 44, No. 2 (April 2008): 10.

6. Wikipedia reports: "The Sarbanes–Oxley Act of 2002 (Pub.L. 107–204, 116 Stat. 745, enacted July 29, 2002), also known as the 'Public Company Accounting Reform and Investor Protection Act' (in the Senate) and 'Corporate and Auditing Accountability and Responsibility Act' (in the House) and more commonly called Sarbanes–Oxley, Sarbox or SOX, is a United States federal law which set new or enhanced standards for all U.S. public company boards, management and public accounting firms. It is named after sponsors U.S. Senator Paul Sarbanes (D-MD) and U.S. Representative Michael G. Oxley (R-OH).

"The bill was enacted as a reaction to a number of major corporate and accounting scandals including those affecting Enron, Tyco International, Adelphia, Peregrine Systems and WorldCom. These scandals, which cost investors billions of dollars when the share prices of affected companies collapsed, shook public confidence in the nation's securities markets."

CHAPTER 6: MCDONALD'S SECRET SAUCE
FOR SUPPLY CHAIN SUCCESS

1. "3PL Management New Tips and Tools," *Operations Leadership Exchange: The Corporate Executive Board*, 2009.
2. Ian R. MacNeil, *Contracts: Instruments for Social Cooperation* (South Hackensack, NJ: F. B. Rothman, 1968).
3. Ibid.
4. O. E. Williamson, "Outsourcing: Transaction Cost Economics and Supply Chain Management," *Journal of Supply Chain Management* 44, no. 2 (2008): 5–16. Blackwell Publishing Inc. Retrieved from http://doi. wiley.com/10.1111/j.1745–493X.2008.00051.x.
5. Kate Vitasek, Jerry Stevens, and Katherine Kawamoto, "Unpacking Outsourcing Governance: How to Build a Sound Governance Structure to Drive Insight vs. Oversight." University of Tennessee, May 30, 2011.
6. Ibid.
7. John F. Love, *McDonald's: Behind the Golden Arches, rev. ed.* (New York: Bantam Books, 1995), relates the widespread practice of the chain restaurant business during the 1950s. It concludes: "Having captive licensees as guaranteed buyers, franchisers needed to do little else than sit back and collect money."
8. This is one of Ray Kroc's most quoted sayings. McDonald's still stands by it, incorporating the language into its web-based I'm Loving It Franchise application, http://www.mcdonalds.com/us/en/our_story/our _history/the_ray_kroc_story.html.
9. Personal interview with Francesca DeBiase by Kate Vitasek and Jeanne Kling, April 2, 2012.
10. Cargill is a private company and is an international producer and marketer of food, agricultural, and financial and industrial products and services.
11. Personal correspondence between Pete Richter and Kate Vitasek, March 22, 2012
12. Personal interview with Gary Johnson by Kate Vitasek, June 2011.
13. Personal interview with Zoran Rancic by Kate Vitasek, June 2011.
14. Personal interview with Midd McManus by Kate Vitasek, Karl Manrodt, and Jeanne Kling, September 14, 2011.
15. Personal interview with Carey Cooper by Kate Vitasek, Karl Manrodt, and Jeanne Kling, October 3, 2011.
16. Personal interview with Jerome Lyman by Kate Vitasek, June 2011.

17. Lopez Foods, http://www.mcdonalds.com/us/en/food/food_quality /see_what_we_are_made_of/meet_our_suppliers/lopez_foods.html.
18. Peter Eisler, Blake Morrison, and Anthony DeBarros, "Fast-Food Standards for Meat Top Those for School Lunches," *USA Today*, December 9, 2009, http://www.usatoday.com/news/education/2009–12 -08-school-lunch-standards_N.htm.
19. Elizabeth Weise, " How McDonald's Makes Sure Its Burgers Are Safe," *USA Today*, December 30, 2009, http://www.usatoday.com/money /industries/food/2009–12-29-mdonalds-burgers-food-safety_N.htm.
20. Personal interview with Ed Sanchez by Kate Vitasek, Karl Manrodt, and Jeanne Kling, November 1, 2011.
21. Personal interview with Mike Ward by Kate Vitasek, Karl Manrodt, and Jeanne Kling, September 21, 2011.
22. Personal interview with Ed Sanchez by Kate Vitasek, Karl Manrodt and Jeanne Kling, November 1, 2011.
23. Personal interview with Francesca DeBiase by Kate Vitasek and Jeanne Kling, April 2, 2012.
24. Personal interview with Pete Richter by Kate Vitasek, Karl Manrodt, and Jeanne Kling, September 7, 2011.
25. Personal interview with John Burke by Kate Vitasek, Karl Manrodt, and Jeanne Kling, October 2, 2011.
26. Personal interview with Eric Johnson by Kate Vitasek, Karl Manrodt, and Jeanne Kling, September 13, 2011.
27. OSI is a global leader that provides supply chain management and freight management services to the foodservice industry.
28. Personal interview with Michael Boccio by Kate Vitasek, Karl Manrodt, and Jeanne Kling, October 28, 2011.
29. Personal interview with Jose-Luis Bretones-Lopez by Kate Vitasek, June 2011.
30. Personal interview with Mark Bendix by Kate Vitasek, Karl Manrodt, and Jeanne Kling, September 9, 2011.
31. Personal interview with Gary Johnson by Kate Vitasek, September 2011.
32. Personal interview with John Burke by Kate Vitasek, Karl Manrodt, and Jeanne Kling, October 2, 2011.
33. Personal interview with Dan Gorsky by Kate Vitasek, June 2011.
34. Personal interview with Devin Cole by Kate Vitasek, Karl Manrodt, and Jeanne Kling, October 12, 2011.
35. Personal interview with Dan Gorsky by Kate Vitasek, June 2011.
36. Personal interview with Chip Klosterman by Kate Vitasek, Karl Manrodt, and Jeanne Kling, September 9, 2011.
37. Personal interview with Gary Johnson by Kate Vitasek, June 2011.
38. This story is discussed in Love, *McDonald's: Behind the Golden Arches*.
39. Ibid.
40. McDonald's 2010 Annual Report, http://www.aboutmcdonalds.com /mcd/investors/annual_reports.html.

41. "McDonald's Tops 2011 Dow Jones Performances," QSRWeb. com, December 28, 2011, http://www.qsrweb.com/article/188494 /McDonald-s-tops-2011-Dow-Jones-performances.

CHAPTER 7: ONE SIZE FITS ALL

1. Roger Dacier and Wesley Thomas, eds., *Back to the River* (Video), a Small Media Large Production, 2010, www.waterforpeople.org.
2. AguaConsult is a small consulting firm that offers safe water technical assistance around the world.
3. Ned Berslin, "Impact over Time," *Water For People Connections* 2, no. 3 (Winter 2009): 2.
4. Eileen Lambert, "Solving Local Problems: India," September 1, 2010, http://www.waterforpeople.org/media-center/stories/solving-local-problems.html.
5. Water For People started projects in more than 40 countries. Over time, it learned that trying to do too much in too many places has diminishing returns.
6. The web site for FLOW is http://watermapmonitordev.appspot.com/.
7. "Mission: Mission, Vision, and Guiding principles," n.d., www.water forpeople.org.
8. The sample agreements are informational as well as legal and filled with photos and friendly explanations of the problem, program, and community expectations. The section dealing with options is almost catalog like, with photos and diagrams of each option, along with technical and pricing information.
9. Personal interview with Daniel Keto by Kate Vitasek, December 2, 2011.
10. Bob Evans, "CIO: Outsourcing Helps His Team Become Strategic," *Information Week*, March 13, 2009.
11. Ibid.
12. Kate Vitasek, Jacqui Crawford, Jeanette Nyden, and Katherine Kawamoto, *The Vested Outsourcing Manual: A Guide for Creating Successful Business and Outsourcing Agreements* (New York: Palgrave Macmillan, 2011).

BIBLIOGRAPHY

CHAPTER 2: P&G'S GAME CHANGER IN OUTSOURCING

Answers.com. "Procter & Gamble." Last modified December 16, 2010. http://www.answers.com/topic/procter-gamble.

Article 13: The Responsible Business Experts. "CSR Best Practice P & G." 2002. http://www.article13.com/A13_ContentList.asp?strAction=GetPublication&PNID=100.

———. "Procter & Gamble: Business Insights." 2002. http://www.article13.com/A13_ContentList.asp?strAction=GetPublication&PNID=100.

Cisco. "Success Stories—Customer Profile Procter & Gamble." 2001. http://www.cisco.com/warp/public/779/ibs/solutions/supply/pgcasestudy1.pdf.

Collins, C. A. "Procter & Gamble PowerPoint Strategic Overview." Scribd.com. Retrieved December 27, 2010, http://www.scribd.com/doc/19594884/Procter-Gamble-Powerpoint-Strategic-Overview.

Corporate Information. "Procter & Gamble Co. (The) Company Snapshot." Last modified December 23, 2010. http://www.corporateinformation.com/company-snapshot.aspx?cusip=742718109.

Donaldson Capital Management. "Procter & Gamble: Defensive, Global, Growth." Last modified March 13, 2008. http://risingdividendinvesting.blogspot.com/2008/03/Procter-and-gamble-defensive-global.html.

Habib, M. "Procter & Gamble Unveils New Sustainability Vision." Procter & Gamble. Last modified September 2010. http://multivu.prnewswire.com/mnr/pg/46415/.

Huston, L. A. "P&G's New Innovation Model." *Harvard Business Review* 84:3 (March 2006). Retrieved December 27, 2010, http://hbswk.hbs.edu/archive/5258.html.

Jones, Lang, LaSalle. "Case Study: Teaming Towards a Sustainable Impact at Proctor & Gamble." , http://www.us.am.joneslanglasalle.com/unitedstates/en-us/pages/casestudydetail.aspx?itemid=1137.

———. "Energy and Sustainability." http://www.us.am.joneslanglasalle.com/unitedstates/en-us/pages/energyandsustainability.aspx?tabindex=3.

Kimes, M. "A Tough Job for P&G's New CEO." CNN Money.com, June 10, 2009. http://money.cnn.com/2009/06/10/news/companies/pandg_mcdonald.fortune/index.htm.

Knol: A Unit of Knowledge. "How Procter & Gamble Survived Through Innovation—A Case Study." 2009. http://knol.google.com/k/how-procter-and-gamble-survived-through-innovation-a-case-study#.

Lafley, A. G. CEO, Chairman. Interviewed by H. B. Paul Mickelman.(n.d.). http://blogs.hbr.org/anthony/2008/05/innovation_advice_from_procter.html;

Lafley, A., & Charan, R. *The Game Changer.* New York: Crown Business, 2008.

Madapati, R. "Procter & Gamble: Organization 2005 and Beyond." ICMR (IBS Center for Management Research. May 21, 2008;Retrieved December 27, 2010, http://www.icmrindia.org/free%20resources/articles/procter1.htm.

Mallen Baker. "The Global Sullivan Principles of Corporate Social Responsibility." Retrieved January 3, 2011, mallenbaker.net: http://www.mallenbaker.net/csr/CSRfiles/Sullivan.html.

MBA Knowledge Base. "Corporate Restructuring Exercises by Procter & Gamble (P&G)." Retrieved December 27, 2010, http://www.mbaknol.com/management-case-studies/corporate-restructuring-exercises-by-procter-gamble-pg/.

Murphy, C. "Procter & Gamble CIO Filippo Passerini: 2010 Chief Of The Year." *Information Week Global CIO*, December 4, 2010. http://www.informationweek.com/news/global-cio/interviews/showArticle.jhtml?articleID=228500182.

Pitman, S. "Procter & Gamble Increases Commitment to Sustainability." Last modified September 30, 2009. http://www.cosmeticsdesign.com/Financial/Procter-Gamble-increases-commitment-to-sustainability.

Procter & Gamble. "Procter & Gamble Releases 11th Annual Sustainability Report." Last modified October 19, 2010. http://www.reliableplant.com/Read/20684/procter-_-gamble-releases-11th-annual-sustainability-report.

Tapscott, D. "Procter & Gamble: Balancing Optimization and Compliance." 2006. Retrieved December 27, 2010,

"Unicef P&G Partner Since 2000." Retrieved December 27, 2010, http://www.unicefusa.org/partners/corporate/procter-gamble.html.

Venable, T. (2005) (2006). William reeves.; Proctor & Gamble's William Reeves—Driving Leading-Edge Service Delivery, 60–65.; Corporate Real Estate Leader; Volume 4, Issue 2; March 2005

Vitasek, K., M. Ledyard, and K. Manrodt. *Vested Outsourcing: Five Rules that Will Transform Outsourcing.* New York: Palgrave Macmillan, 2010.

Vitasek, Manrodt, Wilding, and Cummins. "Unpacking Oliver: 10 Lessons to Improve Collaborative Outsourcing." University of Tennessee, 2010. http://www.vestedoutsourcing.com/resources/whitepapers/

CHAPTER 3: MINNESOTA TURNS I-35W BRIDGE
TRAGEDY INTO TRIUMPH

"Accelerated Construction; Faster Than Ever." *Roads and Bridges* (August 2008). http://www.flatironcorp.com/assets/pdf/08–2008-RoadsandBridges-I-35W(web).pdf.

American Transportation Award. "America's Transportation Awards." Last modified December 16, 2010. http://www.americastransportationaward.org/Default.aspx.

Catalog of Practical Papers. "VIII. Bridge Design and Performance." Retrieved December 13, 2010, http://onlinepubs.trb.org/Onlinepubs/am/bridge.#981038.

Chiglio, J. "I-35 St. Anthony Falls Bridge." *HPC Bridge Views* Issue 52 (November/December 2008). http://test.hpcbridgeviews.com/i52/Article1.asp.

———. "Transportation Task Force." Minnesota Department of Transportation. Last modified November 25, 2008. http://www.dot.state.mn.us/updates/pdf/nov25/Design%20Build%20Best%20Practices.pdf.

———. MnDOT Project Manager. Interview by J. Kling, February 4, 2011.

Chiglio, J., and L. Figg. "The New St. Anthony Falls Bridge." *Aspire* (Winter 2008). http://www.aspirebridge.org/pdfs/magazine/issue_05/I-35W_win08.pdf.

Cho, A. "Mixing Social and Structural Skills, Project Leaders Guided Historic Rebuild in Minnesota." *Engineering News Record*, January 7, 2009. http://enr.construction.com/people/awards/2009/0107-PeterSanderson.asp.

———. "Mixing Social and Structural Skills; Leaders Guided Historic Rebuild Project." *Engineering News Record* (January 7, 2009). http://enr.construction.com/people/awards/2009/0107-PeterSanderson.asp.

DeHaven, T. A. "I-35 Bridge Replacement Design-Build Project." Retrieved December 20, 2010. http://www.pwri.go.jp/eng/ujnr/tc/g/pdf/24/24–7-1thomas%20a.%20dehaven,%20p.e..pdf

Fabyanske, Westra, Hart & Thomson, P.A. "The Construction Law Briefing Paper 05–05." Last modified September 2005. http://www.fwhtlaw.com/files/pdf/New_MN_Statutes_Allow_Design_Build.pdf.

FHWA Office of Innovative Delivery. "P 3 Defined." Retrieved December 26, 2010, http://www.fhwa.dot.gov/ipd/p3/defined/design_build.htm.

Figg, L. *Bridging The Mississippi: The New I-35W Bridge.* Twin Cities, MN: Figg Engineering, 2008.

Figg, L., and A. R. Phelps. "Soaring Across the Mississippi River." *Aspire* (Fall 2008). http://www.flatironcorp.com/assets/pdf/i35_aspire_fall08.pdf.

Flatiron Corporation. "Build the Best; Be The Best." Last modified April 10, 2008. http://www.flatironcorp.com/assets/ProjectSheets/1040-I-35(W)Bridge.pdf.

———. "I-35W (St. Anthony) Bridge." Last modified April 14, 2010. http://www.flatironcorp.com/assets/ProjectSheets/1040-I-35(W)Bridge.pdf.

Foti, J. "He Brings World of Experience to Bridge Project." *Star Tribune* (Minneapolis), November 27, 2007. http://projects.dot.state.mn.us/35wbridge/pdfs/StarTribune1.pdf.

Fountain, H. "Concrete is Remixed with Environment In Mind". *New York Times,* March 31, 2009. http://www.nytimes.com/2009/03/31/science/earth/31conc.html?pagewanted=1&_r=2.

French, C. Professor of Civil Engineering at the University of Minnesota. Interview by J. Kling, February 23, 2011.

———. Professor of Civil Engineering at the University of Minnesota. Interview by J. Kling, February 9, 2011.

"From Tragedy to Triumph." *Engineering News Record* (September 15, 2008). http://www.flatironcorp.com/assets/pdf/09–15-2008-ENR-I-35W.pdf.

Fuhrman, K., and V. Desens. "Fracture Critical Bridge Report In-Depth Study." Minnesota Department of Transportation. Last modified June 2006. http://www.dot.state.mn.us/i35wbridge/pdfs/06fracture-critical-bridge-inspection_june-2006.pdf.

Garrison, T., and L. Evey "Design Build Radio Network." Last modified September 25, 2008. Retrieved March 2, 2011, from www.jackstreet.com: http://www.jackstreet/WCON.DBA.SandersonCFM

Gutknecht, K. MnDOT Public Information. Interview by J. Kling, February 15, 2011.

Hamm, S. "The Bridge to Smart Technology." *Bloomberg Business Week*, February 19, 2009. http://www.businessweek.com/magazine/content/09_09/b4121042656141_page_4.htm.

"I-35W Mississippi River Bridge." *Wikipedia*. Last modified November 16, 2010. http://en.wikipedia.org/wiki/I-35W_Mississippi_River_bridge.

"Instructions to Proposers; St. Anthony Falls (35W) Bridge Design Project." Minneapolis: Minnesota Department of Transportation, August 23, 2007.

Johnson Brothers Construction. Retrieved May 5, 2011, from: http://www.johnson-bros.com/index.htm.

Kennedy, T., and P. McEnroe. "Phone Call Puts Brakes on Bridge Repair." *StarTribune* (Minneapolis), August 18, 2007. http://www.startribune.com/local/11593791.html.

Lam, P. T., M. M. Kumaraswamy, and S. T. Ng. "The Multiple Roles of Specifications in Lean Construction." Retrieved December 22, 2010, http://cic.vtt.fi/lean/singapore/Lametal.pdf.

Legus, G., and Olsen, K. *Bridges Don't Fall Down: Stories from the I-35W Bridge Collapse*. Apple Valley: The Snowy Owl Press, 2008.

McCarthy, E. "New Minnesota Bridge's Super Sensors Scan Tragedy Before It Strikes." *Popular Mechanics* (October 1, 2009). http://www.popularmechanics.com/science/4258306.

Miller, P. "Minnesota Counties Begin Design-Build for Highways." Design-Build Board. Last modified October 25, 2010. http://www.designbuildboard.com/2010/10/minnesota-counties-begin-design-build-for-highways-anoka-county-36–7m-project/.

Minneapolis, City of Lakes. "Minneapolis Begins Municipal Consent Process for Swift, Responsible Consideration for New I-35W Bridge." Last modified August 25, 2007. http://www.minneapolismn.gov/mayor/news/mayor_news_20070821newsmayor_mplsmcp.

Minneapolis Regional Labor Federation, AFL-CIO. "Flatiron-Manson Begins Construction of New 35W Bridge." Last modified November 15, 2007). http://www.minneapolisunions.org/mlr2007–11-15_35W_bridge.php.

Minnesota Department of Transportation. "Innovative Contracting Guidelines." Last modified December 2005. http://www.dot.state.mn.us/const/tools/documents/Guidelines_005.pdf.

———. "Flatiron-Manson Proposal." Last modified September 13, 2007. http://www.dot.state.mn.us/i35wbridge/rebuild/award/FlatironManson1.pdf.

———. "Flatiron-Manson Proposal Form 3." Last modified August 27, 2007. http://www.dot.state.mn.us/i35wbridge/rebuild/award/FlatironManson3.pdf.

————. "I35W Bridge Replacement—Rebuild Plans (8/29/07)." Last modified August 29, 2007. http://www.dot.state.mn.us/i35wbridge/rebuild/pdfs /bridge-replacement-overview-aug30.pdf.

————. "Interstate Bridge over I-35W Mississippi." Last modified September 13, 2007. http://www.dot.state.mn.us/i35wbridge/rebuild/award/FlatironManson1. pdf.

————. "Minneapolis I-35W Bridge; Municipal Consent Hearing." Last modified September 20, 2007. http://www.dot.state.mn.us/i35wbridge/rebuild /municipal-consent/slideshow.pdf.

————. "St. Anthony Falls (35W) Design-Build Project Proposal Evaluation Plan." Last modified September 13, 2007. http://www.dot.state.mn.us /i35wbridge/rebuild/award/evaluationplanforposting.pdf.

————. "Technical Review Committee Summary of Findings Ames/Lunda." Last modified September 2007. http://www.dot.state.mn.us/i35wbridge/rebuild /award/AmesLundaeval.pdf.

————. "Technical Review Committee Summary of Findings Flatiron–Manson." Last modified September 27, 2007. http://www.dot.state.mn.us/i35wbridge /rebuild/award/FlatironMansoneval.pdf.

————. "Technical Review Committee Summary of Findings McCrossan." Last modified September 27, 2007. http://www.dot.state.mn.us/i35wbridge /rebuild/award/CMMcCrossaneval.pdf.

————. "Technical Review Committee Summary of Findings Walsh American Bridge." Last modified September 9,2007. http://www.dot.state.mn.us /i35wbridge/rebuild/award/walsheval.pdf.

————. "I-35W Bridge Work Moves Forward." Last modified February 13, 2008. http://www.newsline.dot.state.mn.us/archive/08/feb/13.html#Z1.

————. "Yearly Listing of all Executed Design-Build Contracts." Last modified August 27, 2008. http://www.leg.state.mn.us/docs/2008/mandated/080639. pdf.

————. "Design-Build on I-35 Bridge." Retrieved December 18, 2010. http:// www.dot.state.mn.us/designbuild/35wbrproject.html.

————. "Flatiron-Manson, a Joint Venture." Retrieved December 16, 2010. http:// www.dot.state.mn.us/designbuild/documents/Flatironfactsheet9.5.07.pdf.

————. "I-35 St. Anthony Falls Bridge, Sidewalk Tour and Animations." Retrieved December 20, 2010. http://projects.dot.state.mn.us/35wbridge/ sidewalkTour.html.

————. "Innovative Contracting—Pay for Performance." Retrieved December 22, 2010. http://www.dot.state.mn.us/const/tools/payforperformance.html.

————. "Rebuilding St. Anthony Falls I-35W Bridge." Retrieved December 16, 2010, http://www.americastransportationaward.org/I-35W_Bridge_Final_ Submittal_040510.pdf.

Minnesota Department of Minnesota, Material Management Admin. "St. Anthony Falls (I-35W) Bridge Replacement Project." Last modified October 8, 2007. http://www.admin.state.mn.us/documents/Protest_determination.pdf.

Minnesota Office of the Revisor of Statutes. "2010 Minnesota Statutes 161.3412 Design-Build Authority." (2010). Retrieved December 12, 2010, from : https://www.revisor.mn.gov/statutes/?id=161.3412.

Morrisey, E. "Bridge Collapse Archives." *Edward Morrisey's Captain's Quarters* (blog), Last modified August 2007. http://www.captainsquartersblog.com/mt/archives/cat_bridge_collapse.php.

Nasvik, J. "Bridge to the Future." Concrete Construction. Last modified September 1, 2008. www.concreteconstruction.net/concrete.../bridge-to-the-future.aspx.

National Transportation Board. "Collapse of I-35W Highway Bridge, Minnespolis, Minnesota August 1, 2007." Retrieved December 13, 2010, http://www.ntsb.gov/publictn/2008/HAR0803.pdf.

O'Connell, H. M., P.E., D. R., and P. M. Bergson. "Fatigue Evaluation of the Deck Truss of Bridge 9340." Minnesota Department of Transportation. Last modified March 2001. http://www.lrrb.org/pdf/200110.pdf.

Positively Minnesota, Department of Employment and Economic Development. "Economic Impact of the Collapse of the I-35W Bridge." Retrieved December 16, 2010. http://www.dot.state.mn.us/i35wbridge/rebuild/municipal-consent/economic-impact.pdf.

"Rochester Highway 52 (ROC52) Design-Build Project." *RECO News* (Volume 6, Issue 2). Retrieved December 18, 2010, from The Reinforced Earth Company: http://www.recocanada.ca/files/pdf/V6I2.pdf.

Sanderson, P. Project Manager Flatiron–Manson. Interview by J. Kling, March 4, 2011.

Think Reliability. "Collapse of the I-35 Bridge—August 1, 2007—Cause Map." Retrieved December 15, 2010. http://www.thinkreliability.com/CM-I35.aspx.

Ward, T. P., and D. P. Jackson. . "Paving a New Road: MnDOT Explores Best-Value Design-Build Delivery." *Design Build Dateline Conference Issue* (November 2005). http://www.dot.state.mn.us/designbuild/background/ward.pdf.

CHAPTER 4: U.S. DEPARTMENT OF ENERGY TRANSFORMS WEAPONS WASTELAND TO WILDLIFE SITE

Agency for Toxic Substances and Disease Registry. "Public Health Assessment for Rocky Flats Environmental Technology Site." Last modified May 13, 2005. http://www.atsdr.cdc.gov/HAC/pha/RockyFlats(DOE)/RockyFlatsPHA051305a.pdf.

Alliance for Nuclear Responsibility. "Plutonium 'Triggers' for Nuclear Bombs 2009." 2009. Retrieved November 27, 2010, http://www.ananuclear.org/Portals/0/documents/2009%20Fact%20Sheets/Pits5%20final.pdf.

Aloise, G. D. "Testimony Before the Subcommittee on Energy and Water Development Committee on Appropriations," House of Representatives. United States Accountability Office, March 4, 2009. http://www.gao.gov/new.items/d09406t.pdf.

Cameron, K., and Lavine, M. *Making the Impossible Possible: Leading Extraordinary Performance the Rocky Flats Story.* San Francisco: Berrett-Koehler Publishers, Inc., 2006. CH2M Hill. , http://www.ch2m.com/corporate/

———. "Rocky Flats Closure Project." Kaiser Hill Announces Physical Clean-Up of Rocky Flats Completed; John Corsi; October 13, 2005 ; http://newsroom.ch2mhill.com/pr/ch2m/2005–10-13_201.aspx. Retrieved November 24,

2010, http://www.ch2m.com/corporate/worldwide/assets/ProjectPortfolio/
united_states/RockyFlats.pdf.

———. "Rocky Flats Closure Report." Retrieved December 1, 2010, http://www
.ch2m.com/corporate/worldwide/assets/ProjectPortfolio/united_states
/RockyFlats.pdf.

Colorado Department of Public Health and Environment. "Rocky Flats Public
Exposure Studies Summary of Findings." Retrieved December 4, 2010,
http://www.cdphe.state.co.us/rf/historyofrf.htm.

Corp, E. R. "Rocky Flats National Wildlife Refuge Scoping Project." U.S. Fish
and Wildlife Service. Last modified January 2003. http://www.fws.gov
/rockyflats/Documents/Public%20Scoping%20Report.pdf.

Charles A. Dan and Norman B. Sandlin, "The Rocky Flats Closure Contract:
Applying Contract Reform Initiatives to a Closure Project." WM '01
Conference, February 25–31, 2001. Last modified February 31, 2001.
http://www.wmsym.org/archives/2001/47/47–1.pdf.

"Great Financial Plans for Your Business." *Real Finance* (blog). Retrieved
December 8, 2010, http://www.rfcab.org/index.html

Department of Energy. "Amendment of Solicitation/Modification of Contract."
1995. Retrieved November 30, 2010, http://rockyflats.apps.em.doe.gov
/references/012–1995%20PMs.pdf.

———. "Final Rocky Flats Cleanup Agreement." Last modified July 19, 1996.
http://rockyflats.apps.em.doe.gov/references/003%20-RFCA%20Doc-
FNLRFCA-All.pdf.

———. "Defense Environmental Services." Retrieved December 5, 2010, http://
www.cfo.doe.gov/budget/05budget/content/em/defenvservice.pdf.

———. "Defense Facilities Closure Projects." Retrieved December 5, 2010,
http://www.cfo.doe.gov/budget/03budget/content/closure/closure.pdf.

———. "DOE Rocky Flats Plant: A Guide to Useful Health Related Services."
Retrieved December 1, 2010, http://www.hss.energy.gov/healthsafety/ohre
/new/findingaids/epidemiologic/rockyplant/intro/index.html#back.

———. "Rocky Flats Fire Department 1995 Closeout." Retrieved December 5,
2010, http://www.hss.energy.gov/nuclearsafety/ns/fire/workshop2004/200
4Presentations/06220403.pdf.

"Donald L. Sebec, Radiation Monitor, Testimonial 191–2004." Rocky Flats
Workers Testimonials. Retrieved December 4, 2010, http://www.rockyflats.
us/Testimonials.html.

Fabyanske, Westra, Hart & Thomson, P.A. "The Construction Law Briefing
Paper 05–05." Last modified September 2005. http://www.fwhtlaw.com
/files/pdf/New_MN_Statutes_Allow_Design_Build.pdf.

GAO—Report to Congressional Committees. "Nuclear Cleanup Progress Made at
Rocky Flats, but Closure is Unlikely and Costs May Increase." Last modified
February 2001. http://www.gao.gov/new.items/d01284.pdf.

Hunsberger, K. "Finding Closure." PMI 2006 Project of the Year, Retrieved
December 9, 2010, http://www.pmi.org/en/About-Us/Our-Professional-
Awards/~/media/PDF/Awards/PMN0107_Rockyflats.ashx.

"Instructions to Proposers; St. Anthony Falls (35W) Bridge Design Project."
Minneapolis: Minnesota Department of Transportation, August 23, 2007.

Kaiser Hill Company Rocky Flats Closure Project. "Project Control System, Rev
0, Contract No. DE-AC34–00RF01904." Last modified March 2, 2000.

http://rockyflats.apps.em.doe.gov/references/054-Proj%20Control%20 System-System%20Description.pdf.

Kaiser Hill Company. "Rocky Flats Closure Project Contract No. DE-AC34– 00RF01904." Last modified March 2, 2000. http://rockyflats.apps.em.doe. gov/references/054-Proj%20Control%20System-System%20Description.pdf.

———. "Project Management Plan, Revision 5." Last modified June 30, 2000. http://rockyflats.apps.em.doe.gov/references/039-CPB%20RF/Appendices /sitepmp.pdf.

Kamensky, J. "Who We Are: A Brief History." National Partnership for Reinventing Government, January 1999. Retrieved November 29, 2010, http://govinfo.library.unt.edu/npr/whoweare/history2.html

Miller, P. "Minnesota Counties Begin Design-Build for Highways." Design-Build Board. Last modified October 25, 2010. http://www.designbuildboard. com/2010/10/minnesota-counties-begin-design-build-for-highways-anoka- county-36–7m-project/.

Miller, V. "Flats Museum Envisioned." *Daily Camera*, October 29, 2006. http:// www.dailycamera.com/ci_13066536?IADID=Search-www.dailycamera. com-www.dailycamera.com.

Minnesota Department of Transportation. "Yearly Listing of All Executed Design-Build Contracts." Last modified August 27, 2008. http://www.leg. state.mn.us/docs/2008/mandated/080639.pdf.

Minnesota Office of the Revisor of Statutes. "2010 Minnesota Statutes 161.3412 Design-Build Authority." 2010. Retrieved December 12, 2010, https:// www.revisor.mn.gov/statutes/?id=161.3412.

"Mutual Assured Destruction." Nuclear Files.org, 1998. Retrieved November 29, 2010, http://www.nuclearfiles.org/menu/key-issues/nuclear-weapons /history/cold-war/strategy/strategy-mutual-assured-destruction.htm.

News, B. B. "Kaiser-Hill Lands Rocky Flats Contract." SFGate.com, April 5, 1995. http://articles.sfgate.com/1995–04-05/business/17802637_1_icf- kaiser-international-kaiser-hill-ch2m-hill.

Pen-L Mailing List Archive. "Rocky Flats—a Toxic Mess." Last modified June 30, 2000. http://archives.econ.utah.edu/archives/pen-l/2000m06.5 /msg00131.htm.

Rocky Flats Closure Project. "The Most Dangerous Building in America Ready for Demolition." Retrieved December 1, 2010, http://www.rockyflatssc .org/rfcab_legacy_report.pdf

Rocky Flats Coalition of Local Governments. "Board Meeting Minutes." Last modified November 4, 1999. http://www.ci.broomfield.co.us/RFCLOG /rockyflatsminutes11_4_99.shtml.

"Rocky Flats Plant." *Wikipedia*. Retrieved December 4, 2010, http://en.wikipedia. org/wiki/Rocky_Flats_Plant.

"Rocky Flats Plant Workforce Restructuring Plan." Last modified October 13, 1993. http://www.docstoc.com/docs/638841/Rocky-Flats-Plant-Work-Force- Restructuring-Plan-October.

Rubin, D. K. "CH2MHill Pushes Boundaries, but Relies on Core Values." *Engineering News Record*, March 12, 2007. http://www.ch2m.com/corpo- rate/news_room/assets/ENR_Cover.pdf.

Scott, S. "Procurement Request Authorization." U.S. Department of Energy. Last modified November 30, 1999. http://rockyflats.apps.em.doe.gov/references/013–1999%20PMs-Superstretch.pdf.

Showalter, D. "June Bison Calf, Nursing." Dave Showalter Nature Photography. Retrieved November 29, 2010, http://www.daveshowalter.com/photo.php?id=314&search=bison.

"Statement of Edward R. Simpson, Director of Office of Procurement and Assistance Management, DOE." Energy.gov, August 3, 2009. Retrieved December 5, 2010, http://www.congressional.energy.gov/documents/8–3-09_Final_Testimony_(Simpson).pdf.

Team, C. R. "Making Contracting Work Better and Cost Less." U.S. Department of Energy, February 1994. Retrieved November 29, 2010, https://www.acquisition.gov/sevensteps/library/DOEpb-contracting.pdf

U.S. Department of Energy. "1996 Baseline Environmental Management Report." Retrieved November 29, 2010, http://www.em.doe.gov/bemr/pages/BEMR96.aspx.

———. "Finding Closure ; The Rocky Flats Plant is Transformed from Dangerous Nuclear Wasteland to Community Asset; Kelley Hunsberger; January 2007, Project Management Institute; http://www.pmi.org/About-Us/Our-Professional-Awards/~/media/PDF/Awards/PMN0107_Rockyflats.ashx

———. "Rocky Flats Interagency Agreement." Last modified January 22, 1991. http://rockyflats.apps.em.doe.gov/references/018a-Interagency%20Agreement-SW-A-000011.pdf.

———. "Lessons Learned." Retrieved December 1, 2010, http://rockyflats.apps.em.doe.gov/TOC_Appendix3.aspx.

U.S. Department of Energy Office of Inspector General. "Audit Report: Issues Regarding Fee Structure for Three Environmental Management Projects." Last modified May 2001. http://www.ig.energy.gov/documents/CalendarYear2001/crb0101.pdf.

U.S. Government Accountability Office. "Nuclear Cleanup: Preliminary Results of the Review of the Department of Energy's Rocky Flats Closure Project." September 22, 2005 (GAO-05–1044R). http://www.gao.gov/products/GAO-05–1044R.

Tuor, N. "Building a Learning Organization." CH2MHill. Last modified October 5, 2005. http://www.efcog.org/wg/im/Events/05%20Fall%20Meeting/Presentations/N_Tuor_KH_EFCOG_LLNL_OCT_05.pdf.

Tuor, N. "Rocky Flats Closure Plant 'Making the Impossible Possible.'" Ch2M-Hill. Last modified October 9, 2007. http://www.rc2007.org/Download/Presentations/Nancy_Tuor.pdf.

Vitasek, K., M. Ledyard, and K. Manrodt. *Vested Outsourcing: Five Rules that Will Transform Outsourcing.* New York: Palgrave Macmillan, 2010.

INDEX